SMUCKER'S. COOKBOOK

A Benjamin Company/Rutledge Book

Library of Congress Catalog Card Number: 75-7805
ISBN: 87502-045-3
Copyright © 1976 by The J. M. Smucker Company
All rights reserved
Prepared and produced by Rutledge Books
Published by The Benjamin Company, Inc.
485 Madison Avenue
New York, New York 10022
Printed in the United States of America
First Printing: January 1976

CONTENTS

GUIDELINES TO BUYING
SMUCKER'S PRODUCTS

10-ounce jar jelly = 1 cup
12-ounce jar jam, preserves = 1 cup
18-ounce jar jam, jelly, preserves = 1½ cups
2-pound jar jam, jelly = 2¾ cups

5-ounce jar nuts in syrup = ½ cup
6-ounce jar topping = ½ cup
12-ounce jar topping = 1 cup
18-ounce jar topping = 1½ cups

12-fluid-ounce bottle fruit syrup = 1½ cups

11-ounce jar Cider Apple Butter = 1 cup
16.5-ounce jar Cider Apple Butter = 1½ cups
28-ounce jar Cider Apple Butter = 2½ cups

28-ounce jar Spiced Apple Butter = 2½ cups

HOW IT ALL BEGAN

How does a cookbook find its beginning? This one can trace its origin to the year 1800, when Johnny Appleseed wended his way through Ohio planting apple seeds and tending the young orchards for early settlers. He was a missionary, Jonathan Chapman, but it was his apple trees that became legend. They reportedly still flourish today, as does the company that was founded because the trees were there.

In 1897, Jerome M. Smucker began operating a small custom cider mill for himself and nearby farmers in Orrville, Ohio, a town with a population of 1,200. So the company began, in one of Ohio's richest agricultural districts, the rolling hills of Wayne County. Soon he added an apple butter-boiling operation to the cider mill. The product was made with a recipe his grandfather David Smucker brought from south-central Pennsylvania.

The J. M. Smucker Company headquarters are still located in Orrville, Ohio. A large modern plant stands on the site of the original mill at the corner of Walnut Street and Strawberry Lane. Today, third and fourth generation members of the Smucker family direct the company, which is the largest processor of jams, jellies, preserves, toppings, and fruit syrups in the United States. All of the Smucker family, as well as their employees, are dedicated to the first rule of the business established by the founder—provide quality products at a fair price. The quality record is a justified source of pride. Smucker's has its own fruit-processing facilities throughout the United States to assure a supply of uniform high-quality fruits.

More than 25 years ago, Smucker's preserve and jelly operations were voluntarily placed under USDA inspection, a step which authorized use of the government's highest designation of quality: U.S. Grade A Fancy.

There are no preservatives or artificial colorings in Smucker preserves, jellies, jams, syrups, and fruit butters. (There are two exceptions—cinnamon-apple jelly and mint-apple jelly. Additions to these are allowed by the FDA's Standards of Identity.)

Smucker's Cookbook introduces you to the versatility of cooking with preserves, jellies, toppings, and fruit syrups. Recipes are designed for both the novice and culinary expert. Appetizers through desserts are presented.

"A Nation of Munchers" is an intriguing array of hors d'oeuvres, cookies, and snacks. On to "Heart of the Meal" for lamb, pork, beef, and chicken entrées that are presented with flavorful glazes, sauces, and stuffings. "Staff of Life" offers breads to start the day, to serve as meal accompaniments, or to enjoy during the coffee hour and at tea time. From "Something on the Side," select fruit and vegetable salads, vegetables with glazes and sauces, chutneys, and salad dressings. "A Bevy of Beverages" offers refreshments ranging from party-time punches to children's treats to beautiful hot and cold combinations to please all! "Happy Endings," designed for all dessert devotees, is filled with delicious pies, cakes, tarts, trifles, puddings, and sauces.

Collected here are time-honored favorites as well as imaginative new recipes to challenge the creative cook.

A NATION OF MUNCHERS

What do you do with a family of all-day snackers? Give them something worth eating—protein-rich little meatballs, crispy chicken chunks, tasty cheese snacks. Or, for those with a sweet tooth, here are cookies enough to fill a hundred cookie jars. And the sweetest thing about all these goodies is Smucker's.

APPETIZER MEATBALLS

about 50 meatballs

1 pound ground beef
¾ teaspoon salt
2 tablespoons finely minced
   onion
½ cup fresh bread crumbs
¼ cup milk

All-purpose flour
2 tablespoons butter or
   margarine
1 cup Peach Preserves
¼ cup prepared horseradish
2 teaspoons dry mustard

Combine ground beef, salt, and onion. Combine bread crumbs and milk and add to meat mixture. Toss lightly until well blended. Form mixture into tiny meatballs about ¾ inch in diameter. Roll meatballs lightly in flour. Heat butter in skillet and brown meatballs well on all sides. Drain off excess fat. Combine preserves, horseradish, and dry mustard; blend until smooth. Add to meatballs in skillet; reduce heat and simmer 8 to 10 minutes, stirring occasionally, until all meatballs are glazed. Serve from a chafing dish or over a candle warmer.

Good Idea: For a change in flavor, omit preserves, horseradish, and dry mustard, and heat meatballs with a combination of ½ cup Sweet Orange Marmalade, 1½ teaspoons curry powder, and ⅛ teaspoon onion salt.

DRESSED-UP CHEESE DOLLARS

7 to 8 dozen

½ pound sharp Cheddar
   cheese, grated
1 cup butter or margarine,
   softened

2 cups sifted all-purpose
   flour
¾ to 1 cup Blackberry Jelly

In a bowl, combine cheese and butter. Cream together until blended. Add flour gradually, mixing with a spoon until all ingredients are well blended. Refrigerate until firm. Form into 3 rolls, each 1 inch in diameter. Wrap in waxed paper. Refrigerate several hours or overnight. Preheat oven to 425° F. With a sharp knife, cut cheese rolls into slices about ¼ inch thick. Place ½ inch apart on ungreased baking sheets. Bake 8 to 10 minutes, or until lightly browned. Cool 10 minutes. To serve, spread one dollar with jelly, top with second dollar.

Opposite: Appetizer Meatballs, Dressed-up Cheese Dollars, Raspberry Frost (page 86)

CHEESE ROLL-UPS

18 servings

These are great lunchtime snacks for a child, especially if you are having trouble tempting his appetite

9 thin slices white bread
½ cup grated sharp
    Cheddar cheese
½ cup Cider Apple Butter

½ teaspoon prepared
    mustard
1 tablespoon butter or
    margarine, melted

Trim crust from bread; roll each slice with rolling pin until very thin, to prevent cracking. Cut each slice in half. Combine cheese, apple butter, and mustard. Spread mixture on bread slices. Roll up and fasten with wooden toothpicks. Place on baking sheets; brush with melted butter. Bake 10 to 12 minutes in a 450° F. oven, or until cheese has melted and bread is lightly browned.

SAVORY PUFFS

60 to 70 snacks

Vary the taste of these by varying the jam you use—almost any flavor complements the nutlike cheese

1 cup water
½ cup butter or margarine
1 cup sifted all-purpose flour
½ teaspoon salt

4 eggs
1 cup grated Swiss cheese
¾ to 1 cup Seedless Boysen-
    berry or Blackberry Jam

Preheat oven to 400° F. In medium-size saucepan, bring water to a boil. Add butter. When butter is melted, add flour and salt all at once. Reduce heat and stir vigorously until mixture leaves the sides of the pan and begins to gather into a ball. Remove from heat and add eggs, one at a time, beating vigorously after each addition. Continue beating until mixture has a satin sheen. Stir in cheese. Drop by small teaspoonfuls onto baking sheets, about 1 inch apart. Bake 15 to 18 minutes, or until golden brown. Cool. Cut a small slit in the side of each puff and put about ½ teaspoon of jam inside. Serve immediately.

Good Idea: These puffs freeze beautifully. After baking, cool puffs, then freeze. When ready to serve, reheat, uncovered, in a 350° F. oven 3 to 5 minutes. Slit, fill, and serve immediately.

PEACHY COTTAGE DIP

about 1½ cups

1 cup small-curd creamed
  cottage cheese
½ cup Peach Preserves

½ teaspoon ground ginger
¼ teaspoon ground tumeric
¼ cup mayonnaise

Combine all ingredients. Refrigerate at least 2 hours before serving to allow flavors to blend.

Good Idea: Chunks or slices of raw fruit—apples, pears, bananas—are excellent with this. Or use melba toast rounds or small cheese crackers as dippers.

FRUITED CHEESE HALFMOONS

12 servings

A delicious, quick-and-easy standby for any occasion—keep a can of date-nut bread in the cupboard for these

1 (3-ounce) package cream
  cheese, softened
1 tablespoon milk

1 can date-nut bread, cut
  into 12 slices
3 tablespoons Sweet
  Orange Marmalade

In a bowl, blend cream cheese and milk. Spread on slices of date-nut bread. Spread marmalade over cream cheese. Cut each slice in half for serving.

SWEET-AND-SAVORY SAUSAGE BALLS

50 appetizers

Easy to make the day before—refrigerate, then reheat just before serving

1 pound bulk pork sausage
1 cup Cider Apple Butter
½ cup English Style Orange
  Marmalade

3 tablespoons lemon juice
¼ teaspoon salt
½ teaspoon ground ginger

Form sausage meat into balls about ¾ to 1 inch in diameter. Place in a shallow baking pan. Bake 15 minutes in a 400° F. oven, or until thoroughly cooked. Drain on paper towels. Combine remaining ingredients and heat over low heat until marmalade is melted. Add sausage balls and simmer 15 minutes. Serve hot from chafing dish or over a candle warmer.

MONTE CARLO SPECIALS

4 sandwiches

Here's a hearty, substantial sandwich with a touch of elegance—great for lunch or at snack time

8 slices white bread
½ cup Currant Jelly
4 slices cooked turkey
4 slices Swiss cheese
4 slices cooked ham

2 eggs, lightly beaten
½ cup milk
¼ teaspoon salt
2 tablespoons butter or
  margarine

Spread 4 slices of bread with jelly; add slices of turkey, cheese, and ham. Top with remaining bread slices. In a shallow dish, combine eggs, milk, and salt; beat with a fork until well blended. Dip sandwiches in egg mixture, coating bread well on both sides. Melt butter in skillet over medium heat. Cook sandwiches on both sides until golden brown. Serve warm with additional jelly.

SWEET-AND-SOUR WIENER BITES

about 40 snacks

¾ cup prepared mustard
1 cup Currant Jelly

2 tablespoons sweet pickle
  relish
1 pound frankfurters

In a saucepan, combine mustard, jelly, and relish. Heat over very low heat, stirring constantly, until mixture is hot and well blended. Slice frankfurters diagonally into bite-size pieces. Add to sauce and heat thoroughly. Serve from a chafing dish or over a candle warmer.

Good Idea: For a change in flavor, omit the mustard and combine the jelly and pickle relish with about ¾ cup chili sauce.

DUNKERS' DELIGHT

12 servings

1 cup Pineapple Preserves
¼ cup prepared mustard
¼ cup prepared horseradish
1 to 1½ pints cooking oil
6 whole chicken breasts,
  skinned and boned

2 eggs, well beaten
1 cup water
1½ teaspoons salt
3 tablespoons sesame seed
1 cup all-purpose flour

In a saucepan, combine preserves, mustard, and horseradish. Heat over low heat until well blended. Keep sauce warm. Fill a skillet no more than half full of oil; heat oil to 375° F. Cut chicken into 1- × 1½-inch pieces. Combine eggs, water, salt, sesame seed, and flour. Dip chicken pieces into batter, draining off excess. Place in oil. Fry 3 to 5 minutes, or until golden brown. Drain on paper towels. Keep warm in warm oven. Dip into reserved sauce.

Good Idea: Bring these hot to a snack table if you like; keep the sauce hot over a candle warmer.

GRAPE-BRAN SQUARES

3 dozen

Crunchy and chewy, these are delicious any time, but a favorite of those who like something sweet at breakfast

½ cup shortening
⅓ cup sugar
½ cup dark corn syrup
1 egg
1 tablespoon grated orange
  peel

¾ cup all-bran cereal
2 cups all-purpose flour,
  stirred before measuring
¼ teaspoon baking soda
½ teaspoon salt
½ cup Grape Jam

Preheat oven to 375° F. Grease a 9-inch square baking pan. Cream shortening and sugar together until light and fluffy. Stir in corn syrup, egg, and grated orange peel; beat thoroughly. Stir in cereal. Sift together flour, baking soda, and salt; stir into mixture. Blend thoroughly. Spread half of dough in bottom of prepared pan. Spread jam over top of dough. Between two pieces of waxed paper, flatten remaining dough into a 9-inch square. Remove one piece of paper; place dough over top of jam and remove second piece of paper. Bake 30 minutes, or until done. When cool, cut into 1½-inch squares.

Good Idea: If orange is a flavor favorite of yours, substitute Sweet Orange Marmalade for the Grape Jam in this recipe.

GRANDMOTHER'S JELLY COOKIES *about 3 dozen*

1 cup butter or margarine,
    softened
1½ cups sugar
1 egg
1½ teaspoons vanilla
    extract

3½ cups all-purpose flour,
    stirred before measuring
1 teaspoon salt
½ to ¾ cup Red Raspberry
    Jelly

In a large bowl, cream together butter and sugar until light and fluffy. Add egg and vanilla; beat well. Stir in flour and salt; mix well. Stir (if batter gets too hard to handle, mix with hands) to make a smooth dough. Refrigerate about 2 hours. Preheat oven to 375° F. Lightly grease baking sheets. On a lightly floured board, roll out half of dough to about a ⅛-inch thickness. Cut with a 2½-inch cookie cutter. Roll out remaining dough; but cut with a 2½-inch cutter with a hole in the middle. Place on baking sheets. Bake 8 to 10 minutes, or until lightly browned. Cool about 30 minutes. To serve, spread jelly on plain cookie; top with a cookie with a hole.

14

JELLY-NUT THUMBPRINTS *about 2 dozen*

½ cup butter or margarine
½ cup firmly packed light
    brown sugar
1 egg
1½ cups all-purpose flour,
    stirred before measuring

1 egg white, lightly beaten
1 cup finely chopped nuts
¾ to 1 cup Strawberry, Black
    Raspberry, or Cherry Jelly

Cream butter and sugar together until light and creamy. Beat in egg. Stir in flour and mix until thoroughly blended. Refrigerate dough to chill slightly, about 1 hour. Preheat oven to 350° F. Grease baking sheets. With floured hands, roll dough into balls 1 inch in diameter. Dip balls into egg white, then roll in chopped nuts. Place cookies 2 inches apart on baking sheets. With a thimble, the handle of a wooden spoon, or your thumb, make a depression in center of each cookie. Bake 10 to 12 minutes, or until lightly browned. Cool cookies on rack. If centers have risen during baking, press down again while cookies are hot. When cool, fill centers with jelly.

Opposite: Grandmother's Jelly Cookies, Jelly-Nut Thumbprints

SANDBAKKELSE

about 2 dozen

Make these buttery Norwegian cookies in pans purchased in hardware or specialty stores, or use 2½-inch tart or muffin pans

1 cup butter or margarine, softened	2 cups all-purpose flour, stirred before measuring
1 cup sugar	½ cup finely chopped blanched almonds
1 egg	1 cup Strawberry Preserves

Preheat oven to 350° F. Grease and lightly flour sandbakkelse pans. In a medium bowl, cream together butter and sugar until light and fluffy. Beat in egg. Stir in flour and almonds; mix until thoroughly blended. Press mixture onto bottom and sides of prepared pans, using about 2 tablespoonfuls of mixture per cup and making a ⅛- to ¼-inch layer. Cut off top edges evenly. Bake 15 to 20 minutes, or until lightly browned. Turn pans upside down on a cooling rack and let stand until cooled slightly. Tap pans lightly to loosen cookies; finish cooling on rack. Fill centers with about 2 teaspoons preserves.

Good Idea: For a fancy dessert, fill cookies with whipped cream flavored with almond extract, and top with a dab of preserves.

CHEWY CHERRY BARS

2 dozen

½ cup butter or margarine, softened	1 cup all-purpose flour, stirred before measuring
1 cup firmly packed brown sugar	1 teaspoon baking powder
½ teaspoon almond extract	1 cup quick-cooking oats
	½ cup Cherry Preserves

Preheat oven to 350° F. Grease an 8-inch square baking pan. Cream together butter and brown sugar. Add almond extract. Combine flour and baking powder. Stir in oats. Add flour mixture to creamed mixture. Mix until crumbly. Reserve 1 cup of mixture. Firmly pat remaining crumbs into prepared pan. Spread with preserves, leaving a ¼-inch border along the edges. Top with reserved crumbs. Pat lightly. Bake 30 to 40 minutes, or until browned. Cool. Cut into 1½- × 2-inch bars.

MARMALADE SQUARES

16 squares

2 tablespoons shortening
¼ cup sugar
¼ cup honey
2 eggs
⅔ cup Sweet Orange
  Marmalade
1 cup whole wheat cereal
  flakes

⅔ cup all-purpose flour,
  stirred before measuring
1 teaspoon baking powder
½ teaspoon salt
½ cup finely chopped
  almonds (optional)

Preheat oven to 375° F. Grease an 8-inch square baking pan. Cream shortening and sugar together until light and fluffy. Stir in honey. Add eggs, one at a time, beating thoroughly after each addition. Stir in marmalade and cereal. Sift together flour, baking powder, and salt; stir into mixture. Blend well. Fold in almonds. Spread dough evenly in bottom of pan. Bake 30 to 35 minutes, or until golden brown. Cool, then cut into 2-inch squares.

FRUIT SQUARES

16 squares

½ cup butter or margarine,
  softened
½ cup confectioners sugar
2 eggs, separated
1 cup all-purpose flour,
  stirred before measuring
2 teaspoons grated lemon peel

½ cup sugar
1 tablespoon lemon juice
½ cup Red Raspberry
  Preserves
½ cup finely chopped
  pecans

Preheat oven to 350° F. Cream together butter and sugar. Beat in egg yolks. Stir in flour and lemon peel; mix until thoroughly blended. Pat mixture evenly in bottom of an 8-inch square baking pan. Bake 10 minutes. Remove from oven. Beat egg whites until foamy. Gradually add sugar; continue to beat until mixture stands in stiff peaks. Beat in lemon juice. Spread preserves over top of partially baked dough. Spread egg white mixture over preserves, bringing mixture up to edges of pan and sealing. Sprinkle top with pecans. Bake 25 minutes longer, or until meringue is lightly browned. Cool in pan. Cut into 2-inch squares for serving.

THIMBLE BITES

These good little melt-in-your-mouth sweets have been favorites in American kitchens for more than 200 years

1 cup butter or margarine,
  softened
½ cup sugar
4 egg yolks
1 teaspoon vanilla extract

2 cups all-purpose flour,
  stirred before measuring
½ cup Grape Jam or
  Apricot or Cherry Preserves

In a medium bowl, cream butter and sugar together until light and fluffy. Beat in egg yolks and vanilla. Stir in flour until well blended. Refrigerate dough about 1 hour. Preheat oven to 375° F. With floured hands, roll dough into 1-inch balls. Place cookies about 1½ inches apart on ungreased baking sheets. Using a lightly floured thimble, press a small indentation into the top of each cookie; fill with jam or preserves. Bake 10 to 15 minutes. Cookies should brown only on bottoms. Remove cookies from baking sheets immediately; cool on wire rack.

18

GRAPE-NUT TRIANGLES

4½ dozen

1½ cups all-purpose flour,
  stirred before measuring
½ teaspoon baking powder
⅛ teaspoon salt
¾ cup sugar
½ cup butter or margarine
1 egg

½ teaspoon vanilla extract
1 tablespoon milk
½ cup Grape Jelly
¼ cup chopped pecans
¼ cup flaked coconut
Confectioners sugar

Into a medium mixing bowl, sift together flour, baking powder, salt, and sugar. With a pastry blender or two knives, cut butter into mixture to the consistency of cornmeal. Combine egg, vanilla, and milk; add to crumb mixture and mix until well blended. Refrigerate dough 2 hours. Combine jelly, pecans, and coconut. Let set until ready to use. Preheat oven to 350° F. Lightly grease baking sheets. On a floured board, roll out half the dough at a time to about a ⅛-inch thickness. Cut into 2-inch squares. Place about ½ teaspoonful of jelly mixture in center of each square. Fold into a triangle, pressing edges together. Repeat with remaining dough. Place triangles on baking sheets. Bake 10 minutes, or until lightly browned. Remove to rack to cool. When cool, sprinkle with confectioners sugar.

OLD-FASHIONED COOKIES

6 *dozen*

1 cup butter or margarine
2 cups firmly packed light brown sugar
1 egg
1 teaspoon vanilla extract
4½ cups all-purpose flour, stirred before measuring

1 teaspoon baking powder
½ teaspoon baking soda
¼ teaspoon salt
1 cup dairy sour cream
Granulated sugar
¾ to 1 cup Black Raspberry or Cherry Jelly

Cream butter and sugar together until light. Beat in egg and vanilla. Sift flour, baking powder, baking soda, and salt together. Add to creamed mixture alternately with sour cream, beginning and ending with dry ingredients. Refrigerate dough 1 hour. Preheat oven to 375° F. Grease baking sheets. On floured board, roll dough to ¼-inch thickness. Cut into 2½-inch rounds. Place on baking sheets. Sprinkle with sugar. Dent center of each cookie slightly. Bake 10 to 12 minutes. Remove immediately to wire rack to cool. When cooled, fill indentation in each cookie with about ½ teaspoon jelly.

PECAN CUPS

3½ *dozen*

1½ cups all-purpose flour, stirred before measuring
½ teaspoon baking powder
½ cup butter or margarine
3 tablespoons milk

2 eggs
¾ cup finely chopped pecans
¾ cup Butterscotch Flavor Topping

Preheat oven to 350° F. In a medium bowl, combine flour and baking powder. With a pastry blender or two knives, cut butter into mixture to the consistency of coarse crumbs. Sprinkle milk over top and mix well. Using 1¾-inch muffin cups, place 2 teaspoonfuls dough in each cup. With fingers, press dough against bottom and sides of muffin cups, bringing dough up as far as possible to the top edge. Beat eggs. Stir in pecans and topping. Place about 1½ teaspoonfuls pecan mixture in each dough-lined cup. Bake 25 minutes, or until mixture is set. Remove from oven and cool.

Good Idea: If using 2½-inch muffin cups, place 1 tablespoonful dough in each cup. Press dough about halfway up the sides of the cups, then fill with about 1 tablespoonful of pecan mixture. Bake about 30 to 35 minutes, or until set. This will make 2 dozen larger tarts.

JENNIE'S SPECIAL LADYFINGERS   *2 dozen*

1 (3-ounce) package cream
  cheese, softened
¼ cup Blackberry Jam

2 dozen ladyfingers
Confectioners sugar

Combine cream cheese and jam and blend thoroughly. Split ladyfingers; spread bottom halves with jam mixture. Replace tops; sprinkle with confectioners sugar.

Good Idea: For a flavor change, try Apricot Preserves and a little chopped candied ginger blended with the cream cheese.

BERRYBUSH CHRISTMAS COOKIES   *100 cookies*

1 cup butter or margarine
½ cup sugar
1 egg yolk
½ teaspoon salt
2½ cups all-purpose flour,
  stirred before measuring

4 egg whites, at room
  temperature
¼ teaspoon cream of tartar
10 tablespoons sugar
¾ cup ground walnuts
1 cup Blackberry Jelly
1 cup chopped walnuts

Preheat oven to 350° F. Cream butter and ½ cup sugar together until light and fluffy. Stir in egg yolk. Stir together salt and flour; stir into mixture. Pat dough into thin layer in bottom of a 15- × 10- × 1-inch jelly-roll pan. Bake 20 minutes. Beat egg whites with cream of tartar until stiff but not dry. Add 10 tablespoons sugar gradually, continuing to beat until mixture stands in stiff peaks. Fold in ground walnuts. Spread jelly over top of partially baked dough in pan. Spread egg white mixture over top of jelly. Seal edges. Sprinkle meringue with chopped walnuts. Bake 10 to 15 minutes, or until lightly browned and set. When cool, cut into 1 × 1½-inch rectangles.

Good Idea: Serve these with punch at a party. Other flavors of jelly, such as Red or Black Raspberry or Strawberry, are also tasty in these cookies.

HEART OF THE MEAL

When they ask you "What's for dinner?" they're inquiring about the main dish. Here are dozens of delightful answers—new ways with beef, pork, and lamb, and with poultry and fish as well, for family and company-coming meals all year around. The something-special secret of all these great dishes? Smucker's!

APRICOT CHICKEN
4 servings

Chicken and fruit preserves make great partners—here is a particularly flavorful way to combine them

½ cup Apricot Preserves
2 tablespoons soy sauce
1 tablespoon lemon juice
¼ cup minced onion

1 tablespoon chopped
   parsley
⅛ teaspoon oregano
1 broiler-fryer, cut into
   serving pieces

In a flat glass or china dish or in a mixing bowl, combine preserves, soy sauce, lemon juice, onion, parsley, and oregano. Add chicken pieces and turn several times, coating them well with sauce. Refrigerate overnight, turning pieces several times. Remove from sauce and place in a single layer in a baking pan. Bake, uncovered, in a 375° F. oven 45 to 50 minutes, or until chicken is tender and lightly browned. Brush with sauce several times during cooking. Brush remaining sauce on chicken just before serving.

Good Idea: This is particularly nice with hot cooked rice. The sauce tops the rice and adds to the tastiness.

SAUCY CHICKEN
3 to 4 servings

½ cup soy sauce
½ cup ketchup
½ cup Sweet Orange
   Marmalade

½ cup water
1 broiler fryer, cut into
   serving pieces

In a large glass or china bowl, combine soy sauce, ketchup, marmalade, and water. Add chicken pieces. Refrigerate for 3 to 4 hours, or overnight, turning chicken pieces occasionally. Remove chicken and place in a single layer, skin side up, in a baking pan. Brush with sauce. Bake, uncovered, in a 375° F. oven 45 to 50 minutes, or until chicken is tender. Brush with sauce several times during cooking. Serve remaining sauce with chicken.

Good Idea: This sauce is excellent brushed over hamburger patties, or used as a sauce to heat up meatballs or thin slices of leftover roast pork.

SAUCES FOR BROILED CHICKEN

Here are two good sauces—use either of them to turn a plain broiled chicken into a feast

½ cup butter or margarine
1 teaspoon cornstarch
1 teaspoon grated lemon
  peel
¼ cup lemon juice

⅓ cup Pineapple Preserves
2 tablespoons finely
  chopped onion
1 teaspoon soy sauce
¼ teaspoon dried thyme

Melt butter in saucepan. Add cornstarch and blend. Add remaining ingredients; cook 5 minutes over low heat, stirring constantly. Use to brush chicken during last 5 minutes of broiling time. Serve remainder as a sauce with the chicken. Makes about 1 cup.

1 cup Currant Jelly
¼ cup frozen orange juice
  concentrate
1½ teaspoons cornstarch

1 teaspoon dry mustard
2 or 3 drops hot pepper
  sauce
1 tablespoon cold water

Heat jelly and orange juice concentrate over low heat. Add cornstarch, dry mustard, hot pepper sauce, and water. Cook, stirring constantly, until sauce thickens. Use to brush chicken during last 5 minutes of broiling time. Serve remainder as a sauce with the chicken. Makes about 1 cup.

PINEAPPLE-GLAZED CHICKEN WITH CORNBREAD STUFFING

4 servings

1 (7-ounce) package corn-
  bread stuffing mix
⅓ cup Pineapple Preserves
1 tablespoon water

4 chicken drumsticks and
  thighs
½ teaspoon salt
⅛ teaspoon pepper

Prepare stuffing mix according to package directions. Spoon into a lightly greased 2-quart casserole or baking dish, forming a mound. Combine preserves and water. Season chicken with salt and pepper; brush with preserves. Arrange chicken, skin side down, around stuffing mound so that legs extend over stuffing. Bake, uncovered, in 400° F. oven 30 minutes; turn chicken and baste again with preserves. Bake 30 minutes longer, or until chicken is browned and glazed.

CHERRY-ROASTED CHICKEN

4 servings

1 (5-ounce) package brown and wild rice mix
1/3 cup Cherry Preserves
1/2 cup chopped celery
1 broiler-fryer (3 pounds)
2 tablespoons butter or margarine, melted

1/4 cup minced onion
1 1/2 teaspoons curry powder
1 cup Cherry Preserves
1 teaspoon grated orange peel
1/4 cup orange juice

Cook rice mix according to package directions. Add 1/3 cup preserves and celery and mix well. Stuff chicken with rice mixture; close openings, tie drumsticks to tail, and tuck wings under back. Place breast side up on rack in shallow roasting pan. Brush with half the melted butter. Roast uncovered in 375° F. oven 1 hour. While chicken is roasting, cook onion in remaining butter until tender. Add curry powder and blend. Add remaining 1 cup preserves, grated orange peel, and orange juice. Simmer 2 minutes, stirring occasionally. Roast chicken 30 minutes longer, or until tender, brushing several times with sauce. Heat remaining sauce and serve with chicken and stuffing.

CURRIED ORANGE CHICKEN

4 servings

1 cup English Style Orange Marmalade
1 tablespoon curry powder
1 teaspoon salt

1/2 cup water
1 broiler-fryer, quartered or cut into serving pieces

Butter a 9- × 13-inch baking pan. Combine marmalade, curry powder, salt, and water. Place chicken pieces, cut side down, in pan. Spoon marmalade sauce over chicken and bake, uncovered, in a 350° F. oven 45 minutes. Spoon sauce over chicken several times during cooking. If sauce begins to stick to bottom of pan, add an additional 1/4 cup water. Remove chicken. Pour out sauce and skim off fat. Serve sauce hot with chicken.

Good Idea: Buttered noodles seem just right with this dish. Garnish both noodles and chicken with parsley for a pretty touch. (And always encourage the family to eat the garnish—parsley is rich in vitamins.)

Opposite: Curried Orange Chicken

JE   *4 servings*

re is a new chicken version with a wonderful

1 cup fine dry bread crumbs
3 cups cooking oil
Sour Cream-Apricot Sauce
(follows)

our
egg, well beaten

Cut each chicken breast half into ¾-inch pieces. Coat pieces
with flour, dip into egg, then coat lightly and evenly with bread
crumbs. In a saucepan, heat oil to 375° F. (use a candy thermometer). Pour into metal fondue pan and place directly over
heat. Spear piece of chicken with fondue fork and hold in hot oil
until golden brown. Remove from fondue fork to a dinner fork.
Dip in Sour Cream-Apricot Sauce.

SOUR CREAM-APRICOT SAUCE   *about 1¾ cups*

26   ¾ cup dairy sour cream   3 tablespoons dijon or
     1 cup Apricot Preserves   prepared mustard

In a small bowl, combine all ingredients. Refrigerate to chill well
before serving.

Good Idea: If you like, prepare the chicken, up to the frying
point, in advance. Refrigerate until serving time.

CHERRY-GLAZED CHICKEN   *4 servings*

1 broiler-fryer, cut into   ¼ cup butter or margarine
   serving pieces   ½ cup Cherry Preserves
½ teaspoon salt   2 tablespoons soy sauce
⅛ teaspoon pepper   ½ teaspoon dry mustard

Season chicken pieces with salt and pepper. Melt butter in large
skillet; add chicken and brown on all sides. Combine preserves,
soy sauce, and dry mustard; pour over chicken. Reduce heat.
Cover and simmer about 30 minutes, turning chicken occasionally. Remove cover and simmer 10 minutes longer, spooning
sauce over top of chicken.

MARMALADE DRUMSTICKS

6 servings

These hearty, crunchy, flavorful drumsticks are wonderful take-along food for a family picnic

12 chicken drumsticks
  (about 2½ pounds)
¾ cup Sweet Orange
  Marmalade

2 cups herb-seasoned
  stuffing mix, crushed
½ cup butter or margarine,
  melted

Spread drumsticks with marmalade. Coat evenly with seasoned stuffing. Place in a single layer in a well-greased shallow baking pan. Drizzle butter over chicken. Bake, uncovered, 40 minutes in a 350° F. oven, or until chicken is brown and crusty. Serve warm or cold.

FRUITED RICE WITH CHICKEN LIVERS

4 servings

1 pound chicken livers
¼ cup butter or margarine
2 tablespoons chopped
  onion
1 clove garlic, minced
4 large fresh mushrooms,
  sliced
½ cup chopped green
  pepper
1 cup uncooked rice

2 cups chicken broth or
  bouillon
1 teaspoon salt
⅛ teaspoon pepper
¼ teaspoon dry mustard
½ cup Pineapple Preserves
½ cup blanched almonds
2 tablespoons cooking oil
1 (8-ounce) can pineapple
  chunks, drained

Cut chicken livers in halves or quarters. Melt butter in large skillet; add livers and cook until lightly browned. Remove livers and reserve. Add onion and garlic to butter in pan and cook 1 minute. Add mushrooms and green pepper and cook 2 minutes. Add rice and cook, stirring constantly, 2 minutes more. Add chicken broth, salt, pepper, and mustard. Cover and simmer 20 minutes, or until rice is almost tender. Stir in preserves; simmer 5 minutes more, or until liquid is absorbed and rice is tender. While rice is cooking, brown almonds lightly in hot cooking oil. Add to rice, along with pineapple chunks and reserved chicken livers; toss lightly. Warm mixture gently about 5 minutes to blend all flavors.

AUNT BET'S CHICKEN

4 servings

1 broiler-fryer, cut into
  serving pieces
½ teaspoon salt
¼ cup butter or margarine
1 medium onion, thinly
  sliced

1 rib celery, thinly sliced
½ cup Apple Jelly
¾ cup orange juice
2 tablespoons lemon juice
⅛ teaspoon dried thyme
¼ cup hot water

Sprinkle chicken with salt. Melt butter in large skillet; add chicken and brown on all sides. Remove chicken. Drain off all fat except 2 tablespoons. Add onion and celery and cook over low heat until soft but not browned. Add jelly, orange juice, lemon juice, thyme, and hot water. Cook, stirring constantly, until jelly melts. Return chicken to skillet. Cover and simmer 25 to 30 minutes, spooning sauce over chicken occasionally, until chicken is tender. Remove cover and cook 10 minutes longer.

Good Idea: Serve this with fresh corn fritters and cole slaw with bits of pimiento and green pepper for a good country-style meal.

PEACH-PEPPER CHICKEN

4 servings

1 broiler-fryer, cut into
  serving pieces
½ teaspoon salt
¼ cup butter or margarine
¾ cup Peach Preserves
1 medium onion, sliced

1 tablespoon lemon juice
½ teaspoon ground ginger
1 medium green pepper,
  cut into strips
1 teaspoon cornstarch
2 tablespoons water

Sprinkle chicken with salt. Melt butter in large skillet. Add chicken pieces and brown lightly on all sides. Add preserves, onion, lemon juice, and ginger. Cover and simmer 25 minutes, stirring occasionally. Add green pepper; simmer 5 minutes. Blend cornstarch with water. Stir into mixture and cook until sauce is slightly thickened.

Good Idea: Hot cooked rice seems just right to serve with this. Add a mixed green salad tossed with cubes of cheese.

SAVORY CHICKEN WINGS

6 *servings*

18 chicken wings (3 to 3½
   pounds)
¼ cup butter or margarine
1 onion, sliced
1 cup Pineapple or Peach
   Preserves
½ cup orange juice

⅓ cup soy sauce
1 tablespoon vinegar
1½ teaspoons ground
   ginger
¾ teaspoon salt
¾ teaspoon ground mace
¼ teaspoon dry mustard

Fold tip of each wing under to form a triangle. Melt butter in
large skillet; add wings and onion and cook until wings are brown
on both sides. Combine preserves, orange juice, soy sauce, vinegar, ginger, salt, mace, and dry mustard. Pour over wings. Cover
and simmer about 30 minutes, or until wings are tender, basting
with sauce once or twice. Serve remaining sauce with chicken.

PEACH-GLAZED CHICKEN

6 *to* 8 *servings*

2 broiler-fryers, cut into
   serving pieces
½ teaspoon salt
1 cup Peach Preserves

1 orange, juice and grated
   peel
2 tablespoons minced
   crystallized ginger
1 teaspoon curry powder

Sprinkle chicken with salt. In a saucepan, combine remaining
ingredients; heat over low heat. Place chicken in a shallow
baking pan, skin side down. Brush with preserves glaze. Bake
uncovered in 400° F. oven 25 minutes, basting often with glaze.
Turn chicken over. Bake 30 minutes longer, continuing to baste
with the glaze, until chicken is tender. Brush remaining glaze on
chicken just before serving.

Good Idea: If you don't have crystallized ginger, substitute
½ teaspoon ground ginger—the texture will be different, but the
flavor just as good.

SAUERBRATEN

10 to 12 servings

1½ cups vinegar
1½ cups water
2 bay leaves
12 whole cloves
1½ teaspoons salt
¼ teaspoon pepper
¼ teaspoon ground mace
1 tablespoon sugar
2 large onions, sliced

¼ cup cooking oil
4-pound top or bottom
   round of beef
¼ cup all-purpose flour
3 tablespoons shortening
¾ cup gingersnap crumbs
½ cup Peach Preserves
½ teaspoon ground ginger
   (optional)

In a large saucepan, combine vinegar, water, bay leaves, cloves, salt, pepper, mace, sugar, and onions. Bring to a boil. Cool; add oil. Place meat in a deep glass or china bowl. Pour vinegar mixture over meat. Place in refrigerator and let stand 2 to 4 days, turning meat once a day so it will marinate evenly. Remove meat from marinade and pat dry with paper towels. Dust surface of meat with flour. Melt shortening in heavy dutch oven; add meat and brown well on all sides. Add marinade. Cover tightly and simmer over low heat 3 to 4 hours, or until meat is fork-tender. Turn meat occasionally during cooking time. Remove meat to a hot serving platter and keep warm. Strain marinade. Return 2 cups of the strained marinade to dutch oven. Add gingersnap crumbs and preserves. Simmer until mixture is thick and smooth. Add the ginger, if desired. Cut meat in slices; serve with sauce.

Good Idea: For a different flavor, thicken marinade with 3 tablespoons flour blended into ¼ cup water, rather than with gingersnap crumbs. Stir in ½ cup Grape Jelly. When smooth and thick, stir in ½ cup dairy sour cream. But whichever flavor you prefer, serve potato dumplings or potato pancakes, and red cabbage—they are go-togethers for sauerbraten.

Opposite: Sauerbraten, Red Cabbage (page 79)

CRUSTY GRAPE BURGERS

8 *servings*

1 pound ground beef
1 cup fresh bread crumbs
⅓ cup finely chopped onion
1 egg
⅓ cup ketchup
2 teaspoons prepared
  mustard
1 teaspoon prepared
  horseradish
1 teaspoon salt
⅓ cup Grape Jelly
1 (8- or 8½-ounce)
  package corn muffin mix

Combine ground beef, bread crumbs, onion, egg, ketchup, mustard, horseradish, and salt. Divide into 8 portions. Press mixture into eight 6-ounce custard cups. Place cups on baking sheet and bake in a 400° F. oven 10 minutes. Pour off fat. Spoon jelly over meat. Prepare corn muffin mix according to package directions. Divide batter over jelly in custard cups. Bake 15 to 20 minutes, or until corn bread is lightly browned. Cool slightly. Loosen edges and invert burgers onto plates.

INDIAN MEATBALLS

6 *servings*

1½ pounds ground beef
1 cup fresh bread crumbs
½ cup tomato juice
1½ teaspoons salt
⅛ teaspoon pepper
¼ cup all-purpose flour
2 tablespoons butter or
  margarine
2 medium onions, sliced
1 teaspoon curry powder
½ cup Apple Jelly
1 cup beef broth or bouillon
½ cup tomato juice
Hot cooked rice

Combine ground beef, bread crumbs, ½ cup tomato juice, salt, and pepper. Shape into 36 small balls, 1¼ to 1½ inches in diameter; roll in flour to coat all sides. Melt butter in large skillet; add meatballs and brown on all sides. Remove meatballs and set aside. Remove all but 2 tablespoons of drippings from skillet. Add onions and curry powder to remaining drippings in skillet; cook, stirring often, just until onion is soft. Add jelly, beef broth, and ½ cup tomato juice. Bring to a boil. Return meatballs to skillet. Cover and simmer 20 minutes, stirring often. Serve with hot cooked rice.

Good Idea: Delicious to serve with this dish is Waldorf salad—chopped apple, celery, and walnuts dressed with mayonnaise.

SWEET-AND-SOUR MEATBALLS

6 to 8 servings

1 cup fresh bread cubes
1 cup milk
2 pounds ground beef
⅓ cup finely chopped onion
1 egg
1 teaspoon salt
¼ teaspoon pepper

2 (12-ounce) bottles chili
  sauce
1 cup Grape Jelly
½ cup water
1 cup dairy sour cream
Hot cooked noodles

Soak bread cubes in milk. Combine with ground beef, onion, egg, salt, and pepper. Shape mixture into balls about 1 inch in diameter. In large saucepan, combine chili sauce, jelly, and water; heat to simmering. Drop meatballs into hot sauce and simmer gently about 1 hour. Skim off excess fat. Just before serving, add sour cream to sauce and heat, but do not boil. Serve on a bed of hot cooked noodles.

SNAPPY MEATBALLS

4 to 6 servings

1 pound ground chuck
3 tablespoons milk
1 cup fresh bread crumbs
1 egg, lightly beaten
3 tablespoons finely
  chopped onion
1 teaspoon salt

½ cup gingersnap crumbs
½ cup Pineapple Preserves
2 cups beef broth or bouillon
¼ cup lemon juice
¼ teaspoon ground ginger
Hot cooked rice or noodles

Combine ground chuck, milk, bread crumbs, egg, onion, and salt; mix lightly. Shape mixture into balls, about 1¼ to 1½ inches in diameter. Place in a shallow baking pan. Bake, uncovered, in a 375° F. oven 25 to 30 minutes, or until meatballs are just cooked. While meatballs are baking, combine gingersnap crumbs, preserves, beef broth, lemon juice, and ginger in a skillet or saucepan. Bring mixture to a boil, stirring constantly. Reduce heat to very low. Drain meatballs and add to preserves mixture; simmer gently 10 to 15 minutes, stirring occasionally. Serve with hot cooked rice or noodles.

GLAZED GRAPE MEAT LOAF

6 servings

1½ pounds ground beef
1½ cups fresh bread crumbs
2 eggs, lightly beaten
1 small onion, minced
1½ teaspoons salt
¼ teaspoon pepper

½ cup Grape Jam
½ cup ketchup
1 tablespoon prepared
  mustard
1 teaspoon prepared
  horseradish

In a medium bowl, combine ground beef, bread crumbs, eggs, onion, salt, and pepper; blend well. Combine jam, ketchup, mustard, and horseradish; stir to blend. Add half the jam mixture to meat mixture; blend well. Shape meat into a loaf. Place in a shallow baking pan. Spoon remaining grape mixture over top. Bake, uncovered, in a 400° F. oven 45 to 50 minutes, or until meat is done.

GLAZED BEEF BRISKET

8 to 10 servings

4 to 5 pounds beef brisket
1 medium onion, quartered
8 peppercorns
1 teaspoon salt

¾ cup Apricot Preserves
2 teaspoons lemon juice
1 teaspoon salt
Whole cloves

Place meat in a large kettle and cover with water. Add onion, peppercorns, and 1 teaspoon salt. Cover tightly and simmer 3 to 4 hours, or until meat is tender. Remove meat and place in a shallow baking dish. Combine preserves, lemon juice, and 1 teaspoon salt. Spread half of glaze over top of meat. Stud meat with cloves. Bake, uncovered, in a 350° F. oven 20 to 30 minutes, or until glaze is set. Heat remaining glaze and serve with meat.

Good Idea: This brisket is even better the second day. Serve cold, in thin slices, with the remaining sauce heated, or serve with any of the other sauces for cold meats on page 53. Save the good broth in which the meat was cooked—freeze it, if you like— to be used in soups or stews.

Opposite: Glazed Beef Brisket, Plum Chutney (page 81), Apple Chutney (page 81), Picture-Pretty Bread (page 65), Orange-Pineapple Coleslaw (page 80)

GOURMET BEEF BIRDS

1/3 cup all-purpose flour
1/2 teaspoon salt
1/4 teaspoon pepper
2 pounds top round steak,
   cut 1/2 inch thick
1 1/2 cups fresh bread crumbs
1/4 cup seedless raisins
1/4 cup finely chopped celery
1 cup peeled, finely
   chopped apple

2 teaspoons prepared
   mustard
1/4 teaspoon rubbed sage
1 1/2 teaspoons salt
1/4 cup Crabapple Jelly
3 tablespoons cooking oil
3/4 cup Crabapple Jelly
1/4 cup water

Combine flour, 1/2 teaspoon salt, and pepper. Pound seasoned flour into steak. Cut steak into 6 portions. Combine bread crumbs, raisins, celery, apple, mustard, sage, 1 1/2 teaspoons salt, and 1/4 cup jelly. Divide mixture among pieces of steak. Roll meat jelly-roll fashion; secure with wooden toothpicks or skewers. In a large skillet, heat oil. Add beef birds and brown slowly on all sides. Pour off drippings. Combine 3/4 cup jelly with water and pour over meat. Cover tightly and simmer about 1 1/2 hours, or until meat is tender. Stir occasionally during cooking time and add more water if necessary.

Good Idea: If your market has beef braciole—which is already cut paper thin—it is easier to use, as it does not have to be pounded. These birds also make delicious appetizers—refrigerate overnight, cut into slices about 1/2 inch thick, and secure with a wooden toothpick. They need no sauce.

36

SPICY SHORT RIBS

3 pounds short ribs of beef
1/4 cup all-purpose flour
2 tablespoons shortening
1 cup beef broth or bouillon
1/2 cup Apricot Preserves
2 tablespoons brown sugar
2 tablespoons vinegar

1/4 teaspoon ground allspice
1/4 teaspoon ground
   cinnamon
1/4 teaspoon ground cloves
1 tablespoon cornstarch
1 tablespoon cold water

Remove as much excess fat from ribs as possible. Dust ribs with flour. Melt shortening in a dutch oven or large heavy skillet.

Place ribs in skillet; brown well on all sides. Pour off excess drippings. Combine broth, preserves, brown sugar, vinegar, and spices. Pour over ribs. Cover and cook over low heat about 2½ hours, or until ribs are tender, turning ribs occasionally during cooking time. With a spoon, skim as much fat as possible from top of sauce. Combine cornstarch and water to make a smooth paste. Stir into sauce and cook, stirring, until sauce is clear and lightly thickened.

Good Idea: This is particularly good made a day in advance. Do not thicken. Refrigerate and, when cold, remove all fat from top of sauce and meat. Just before serving, heat, then thicken with cornstarch paste as above. Mashed potatoes are just right with these ribs and their tasty sauce.

CHEESE HIDE-A-WAYS

6 to 8 servings

1 pound ground beef
1 tablespoon brown sugar
2 tablespoons Sweet
   Orange Marmalade
2 tablespoons minced onion
2 tablespoons chopped
   parsley
1 teaspoon dry mustard
½ teaspoon dried savory
¾ teaspoon salt
¼ teaspoon pepper

1 cup soda cracker crumbs
2 eggs, lightly beaten
½ pound pasteurized
   process American cheese
2 tablespoons butter or
   margarine
2 cups dairy sour cream
1 tablespoon brown sugar
2 tablespoons Sweet
   Orange Marmalade
¼ teaspoon dried tarragon

Combine ground beef, 1 tablespoon brown sugar, 2 tablespoons marmalade, onion, parsley, dry mustard, savory, salt, pepper, and cracker crumbs. Add eggs and mix lightly until well blended. Cut half the cheese into 24 small cubes. Insert a piece of cheese into the center of a generous tablespoon of meat mixture. Shape into a ball around the cheese. Repeat until all meat and cubed cheese are used. Melt butter in large skillet. Add meatballs and cook slowly until well browned on all sides. Melt remainder of cheese in the top of a double boiler over hot water. Gradually blend in sour cream. Add 1 tablespoon brown sugar, 2 tablespoons marmalade, and tarragon. Heat. Pour mixture over meatballs. Cover and heat slowly for 5 minutes, but do not boil.

STUFFED CABBAGE

4 *servings*

½ **pound ground beef**
1 **cup cooked rice**
2 **tablespoons minced onion**
½ **teaspoon salt**

4 to 6 **large cabbage leaves**
½ **cup Apple Jelly**
3 **tablespoons lemon juice**
¼ **cup water**

Combine ground beef, rice, onion, and salt. Pour boiling water over cabbage leaves and let stand a few minutes until cabbage is wilted. Drain well. Cut tough core out of cabbage leaves. Divide beef mixture among leaves. Roll cabbage leaf around mixture and secure with wooden toothpick. Place filled rolls in heavy skillet. Combine jelly, lemon juice, and water. Pour over cabbage rolls. Cover and simmer 50 to 60 minutes. Check occasionally and, if necessary, add hot water to prevent cabbage rolls from sticking to skillet.

Good Idea: To remove cabbage leaves easily, cut core out of cabbage to a depth of 3 inches. Place cabbage core side down in boiling water and steam until leaves are loosened. Remove leaves carefully with tongs and drain well before stuffing. For a change in flavor, combine ½ cup Peach Preserves, ½ teaspoon prepared horseradish, 3 tablespoons lemon juice, and ¼ cup water, and use in place of the jelly mixture.

38

TONGUE WITH BLACKBERRY SAUCE

6 *servings*

1 2½- **to 3-pound beef tongue**
1 **onion, studded with 3 cloves**
8 **peppercorns**
1 **bay leaf**
1 **carrot, cut up**

1 **rib celery, with leaves, cut up**
½ **cup Seedless Blackberry Jam**
1 **tablespoon lemon juice**
½ **cup seedless raisins**

Place tongue in kettle and cover with water. Add onion, peppercorns, bay leaf, carrot, and celery. Bring to a boil. Reduce heat; cover and simmer about 3 hours, or until tongue is tender. Remove tongue and remove skin and root end from tongue. Keep warm. Combine jam, lemon juice, and raisins and heat over low heat. Cut tongue in thin slices and serve with sauce.

CURRANT BEEF TONGUE

4 to 6 servings

8 to 12 slices cooked beef
   tongue
½ cup Currant Jelly
⅓ cup dijon or prepared
   mustard

½ teaspoon ground ginger
1 small onion, minced
1 cup water or liquid
   reserved from cooking
   tongue

Arrange tongue slices in a 1- to 1½-quart shallow casserole or baking dish. In a small saucepan, combine jelly, mustard, ginger, and onion. Add water or reserved liquid. Bring to a boil, stirring occasionally. Reduce heat and simmer about 10 minutes. Pour over tongue. Bake tongue, uncovered, in 350° F. oven about 30 minutes, or until slices are heated through. Spoon sauce over tongue occasionally during baking time.

PORK AND PEPPERS

4 servings

4 large green peppers, cut
   into 1-inch squares
1 egg
2 tablespoons all-purpose
   flour
½ teaspoon salt
⅛ teaspoon pepper
1 pound very lean pork, cut
   into 1-inch cubes

½ cup cooking oil
1 small clove garlic, minced
1 cup chicken broth or
   bouillon
2½ tablespoons cornstarch
2 tablespoons soy sauce
¼ cup vinegar
½ cup Pineapple Topping
Hot cooked rice

Place pepper chunks in boiling water 2 to 3 minutes. Drain and reserve. Combine egg, flour, salt, and pepper. Add pork cubes to batter and toss lightly with a fork so that each piece of pork is coated. Heat oil in heavy skillet. Add garlic and cook 1 minute. Add pork and cook until golden brown, about 5 to 6 minutes. Pour off as much oil as possible. Add ⅓ cup of the broth to skillet. Cover and simmer 10 minutes, or until pork is tender. Combine remaining broth, cornstarch, soy sauce, vinegar, and topping. Add to skillet and cook, stirring constantly, until mixture thickens and becomes clear. Stir in reserved green pepper and heat thoroughly. Serve immediately with hot cooked rice.

PORK-AND-PLUM SKILLET

6 *servings*

1 tablespoon cooking oil
2 pounds lean pork, cut into
 1-inch cubes
½ cup chopped onion
¼ cup chili sauce

2 tablespoons soy sauce
1 teaspoon ground ginger
2 tablespoons lemon juice
1 cup Plum Preserves
Hot cooked rice or noodles

Heat oil in large skillet; add pork and brown well on all sides. Add onion and cook just until onion is tender. Add chili sauce, soy sauce, ginger, lemon juice, and preserves; stir lightly. Cover and simmer about 25 minutes, stirring occasionally, until pork is tender. If sauce becomes too thick, add a small amount of water. Serve over hot cooked rice or noodles.

Good Idea: This versatile sauce is also good brushed over chicken as it broils. Or it can be served warm as a sauce for hamburger patties or roast pork.

PORK-KRAUT-APPLE SKILLET

6 *servings*

6 lean pork chops, cut ¾ inch
 thick
1 tablespoon cooking oil
1 teaspoon salt
2 tablespoons butter or
 margarine

3 large onions, thinly sliced
¾ cup Cider Apple Butter
2 pounds sauerkraut,
 drained
1 cup diced, unpeeled
 apple

Remove as much fat as possible from the chops. Heat oil in a large, heavy skillet. Season chops with salt; place in skillet and brown on both sides. Remove chops. Melt butter in skillet; add onions and cook 1 minute. Add apple butter and blend. Return chops to skillet. Cover tightly and simmer about 30 minutes. Combine sauerkraut and diced apple and place on top of chops. Cover and simmer, stirring occasionally, about 20 minutes longer, or until chops are tender.

Good Idea: Add a loaf of good dark bread, with plenty of butter, to make a complete, hearty one-dish meal. If desired, the sauerkraut and apples can be cooked separately, then garnished with additional apples. Serve with pork chops and apple butter.

Opposite: Pork-Kraut-Apple Skillet

CHERRY-STUFFED PORK CHOPS

½ cup Cherry Preserves
¼ cup seedless raisins
¼ cup chopped walnuts
½ cup fresh bread crumbs
1 tablespoon butter or margarine, melted

4 rib pork chops, cut 1½ inches thick, with pockets
½ teaspoon salt
⅛ teaspoon pepper
2 tablespoons cooking oil

Combine preserves, raisins, walnuts, bread crumbs, and butter; toss lightly. Stuff pocket in each chop with part of mixture. Fasten with skewers or wooden toothpicks. Sprinkle chops with salt and pepper. Heat oil in large skillet; add chops and brown on both sides. Remove chops from skillet and place in shallow baking pan. Cover tightly with pan lid or aluminum foil and bake in a 350° F. oven 50 to 60 minutes, or until meat is tender.

PORK CHOPS NEW ENGLAND

6 servings

Here's a new taste combination you'll want to try—apricot and maple turn out to be great flavor partners

½ cup all-purpose flour
½ teaspoon salt
¼ teaspoon pepper
¼ teaspoon dried thyme
6 pork chops, cut ¾ inch thick

3 tablespoons cooking oil
1 cup Apricot Preserves
2 tablespoons maple syrup
¼ cup water

Combine flour, salt, pepper, and thyme. Rub into both sides of pork chops. Heat oil in a large, heavy skillet; add chops and brown on both sides. Combine preserves, maple syrup, and water. Pour over chops. Cover tightly and simmer about 1 hour, or until chops are tender. Serve with the sauce.

PEACHYCOT PORK CHOPS

6 servings

1 tablespoon cooking oil
6 pork chops, cut ½ inch thick
½ teaspoon salt
⅛ teaspoon pepper

½ cup Apricot Preserves
½ cup Peach Preserves
1 tart red apple, chopped
2 tablespoons cider vinegar
¼ cup chopped pimiento

Heat oil in a large, heavy skillet. Season chops with salt and pepper; place in skillet and brown on both sides. Combine preserves, apple, vinegar, and pimiento and pour over chops. Cover tightly and simmer 30 to 40 minutes, or until chops are tender. Turn chops occasionally during cooking time and add a small amount of water if sauce gets too thick. Serve chops with sauce spooned over them.

Good Idea: These chops and their sauce are especially tasty served with hot cooked rice to which have been added 1 tablespoon chopped parsley, 1 tablespoon chopped watercress, and 1 teaspoon snipped chives.

HEARTY PORK AND APPLE BAKE
4 to 6 servings

This rib-sticking cold-weather dish makes a great hit after skating, or after a game or a hike

¼ cup all-purpose flour
1½ teaspoons salt
½ teaspoon pepper
½ teaspoon paprika
2 pounds pork shoulder, cut into 2-inch cubes
3 tablespoons cooking oil
1 large onion, thinly sliced
1 bay leaf, crumbled
1 teaspoon rubbed sage
1 clove garlic, finely chopped

1 cup Cider Apple Butter
4 carrots, peeled and sliced
1 cup diagonally sliced celery
1 small yellow turnip, peeled and thickly sliced
½ cup chicken broth or bouillon
2 tart apples, peeled, cored, and sliced

In a bag, combine flour, salt, pepper, and paprika. Add pork pieces and shake well until pork is covered with flour mixture. Heat oil in a dutch oven. Add pork and brown well on all sides. Remove pork and reserve. Place onion in dutch oven and cook over low heat until golden. Return meat to pan with bay leaf, sage, garlic, and apple butter. Cover and bake in a 325° F. oven 1 hour, or until pork is tender. Add carrots, celery, turnip, and chicken broth. Cover and bake 20 to 25 minutes. Add apples and continue baking at least 10 minutes, or until vegetables and pork are tender.

SPICY PORK ROLL

4 to 6 servings

1 3-pound boneless
   smoked pork shoulder roll
1 medium onion, sliced

1 bay leaf
½ cup Spiced Apple Butter
1 teaspoon dry mustard

Place meat in a large kettle or dutch oven and cover with water. Add onion and bay leaf; bring to a boil. Reduce heat. Cover and simmer 1½ hours, or until tender. Remove meat and place in a shallow baking pan. Remove casing, skin, and excess fat. Combine apple butter and dry mustard. Spread mixture over top of meat. Bake, uncovered, in a 350° F. oven 20 to 30 minutes.

Good Idea: Potatoes boiled in their jackets, panned cabbage, and pickled green beans make this a Pennsylvania Dutch treat all the way. If you're feeling ambitious, make fastnachts (doughnuts) for dessert and listen to the applause!

HILL COUNTRY SPARERIBS

6 servings

44

4 pounds lean spareribs
½ cup chicken broth or
   bouillon
¼ cup soy sauce

¼ cup Sweet Orange
   Marmalade
1 clove garlic, crushed
¼ teaspoon ground ginger
½ teaspoon dry mustard

Cut ribs into serving pieces. Place in a shallow roasting pan. Combine broth, soy sauce, marmalade, garlic, ginger, and mustard; blend well. Pour sauce over ribs; refrigerate 3 to 4 hours, turning ribs several times during marinating time. Cover pan and bake in a 350° F. oven 1 hour and 10 minutes. Uncover and continue baking 20 to 30 minutes, basting ribs occasionally with sauce in bottom of pan, until ribs are brown and tender.

PINEAPPLE SPARERIBS

5 to 6 servings

3 to 4 pounds lean spareribs
1 cup Pineapple Preserves
¼ cup vinegar

½ cup ketchup
1 tablespoon soy sauce

Cut ribs into serving pieces. Arrange half the pieces in a single layer in a roasting pan. In a saucepan, combine preserves, vinegar, ketchup, and soy sauce. Heat, stirring constantly, until well blended. Pour half the pineapple mixture over the layer of ribs. Top with remaining ribs and remaining pineapple mixture. Cover pan and bake in a 350° F. oven 1½ hours. Uncover and continue baking 20 to 30 minutes, basting with the pineapple mixture occasionally, until ribs are brown and tender.

Good Idea: For a change in flavor, try Peach Preserves in this recipe—it's equally good!

SPICY PLUM-SAUCED HAM   *9 to 12 servings*

1 3- to 4-pound canned
  ham
1 cup Plum Preserves
½ cup chutney, chopped

2 teaspoons wine vinegar
1 tablespoon sugar
⅛ teaspoon ground mace

Place ham on rack in a shallow roasting pan. Roast in a 350° F. oven 1½ to 1¾ hours, or until heated through. In a saucepan, combine remaining ingredients and heat over low heat, stirring until well blended. Use to baste ham during last 15 minutes of cooking time. Heat remaining sauce and serve with slices of ham.

45

Good Idea: For smaller hams, decrease roasting time and for larger hams, increase roasting time. The amount of sauce remaining to serve with slices will depend on the size of ham used and on how heavily the ham is basted during cooking time.

STRAWBERRY HAM STEAK   *2 to 3 servings*

2 tablespoons prepared
  mustard
½ cup Strawberry Topping

1 pound fully cooked ham
  steak, cut 1 inch thick

Combine mustard and topping. Place ham steak on rack in broiler pan. Broil about 5 inches from heat, 12 to 15 minutes, turning once and brushing frequently with topping mixture.

HOLIDAY STUFFED HAM

1 12-pound fully cooked
  whole ham
½ cup butter or margarine
1 cup chopped celery
1 cup chopped onions

2 teaspoons grated orange
  peel
1 teaspoon rubbed sage
½ teaspoon pepper
6 slices white bread, cubed
¾ cup Apricot Preserves

Trim off skin and excess fat from ham, leaving about ¼ inch fat. Place in a roasting pan and bake in a 350° F. oven 1½ hours. Melt butter in skillet; add celery and onions and cook gently until tender but not browned. Add grated orange peel, sage, pepper, bread cubes, and preserves. Toss lightly. Remove ham from oven. With fat side of ham up, make deep lengthwise cuts about 2 inches apart in the meat. Press stuffing mixture into the cuts. Return to oven and continue baking 45 to 60 minutes, or until stuffing is cooked and lightly browned on top.

46

Good Idea: For fewer servings, use a half ham. Bake 45 minutes. For the stuffing, make half a recipe, except for Apricot Preserves; use ½ cup. Proceed as above; continue baking for 30 to 45 minutes.

STRAWBERRY-GLAZED HAM

As handsome as it is good to eat, this ham can be the center of the meal on any company-coming occasion

1 5- to 7-pound fully cooked
  smoked butt or shank-half
  ham
1½ cups Strawberry
  Preserves

⅓ cup prepared mustard
¼ cup lemon juice

Trim skin from ham. With a sharp knife, score fat surface, making uniform diagonal cuts about ⅛ inch deep and ¾ inch apart. Place ham fat side up on rack in a shallow roasting pan; bake in a 325° F. oven 1¾ to 2½ hours. Meanwhile, in a small saucepan, combine preserves, mustard, and lemon juice; cook over low heat, stirring, until blended. During last 20 minutes of baking time, brush ham with about ½ cup glaze. Let ham stand 10 minutes for easier slicing. Heat remaining glaze and serve as a sauce for the ham.

HAM SLICE
WITH TOMATO PRESERVES

2 to 3 servings

**1 pound ready-to-eat ham
slice, cut ½ inch thick**
½ cup Tomato Preserves

1 teaspoon dry mustard
**⅛ teaspoon worcestershire
sauce**

Make slashes in fat around edge of ham. Place in a baking pan. Combine preserves, dry mustard, and worcestershire; spread over top of ham. Bake, uncovered, in a 350° F. oven 20 to 30 minutes, or until ham slice is well heated and lightly browned.

SPECIAL SKEWERED LAMB

6 servings

**2 tablespoons butter or
margarine**
**2 large onions, finely
chopped**
½ clove garlic, minced
1 cup Apricot Preserves
¼ cup Apricot Syrup

1 teaspoon salt
⅛ teaspoon cayenne pepper
2 tablespoons curry powder
¼ cup vinegar
**2 pounds lean leg of lamb,
cut into 1-inch cubes**

Melt butter in saucepan. Add onions and garlic; cook until limp. Add preserves, syrup, salt, pepper, curry powder, and vinegar. Cover and simmer gently until well blended. Add lamb cubes to sauce and refrigerate several hours or overnight. Stir occasionally. Drain meat; thread on skewers at least 6 inches long. Place on broiler rack and broil about 10 minutes to desired degree of doneness, turning occasionally. Heat remaining sauce over low heat to serve with meat.

Good Idea: This is especially good cooked over hot coals. Squares of green pepper and button mushrooms can be added to the meat on the skewers, if you like.

CURRANT ROAST LAMB

8 to 10 servings

1 5- to 6-pound leg of lamb, boned
½ cup Currant Jelly
2 cups fresh bread crumbs
¼ cup chopped celery
3 tablespoons butter or margarine, melted

⅛ teaspoon pepper
¼ teaspoon ground allspice
½ teaspoon salt
2 tablespoons brown sugar
1 teaspoon ground nutmeg
Jelly Sauce (follows)

Spread leg of lamb out as flat as possible; spread with jelly. Combine bread crumbs, celery, butter, pepper, and allspice. Spread over jelly. Fold lamb over to enclose stuffing and tie with string every 4 or 5 inches. Place fat side up on a rack in a shallow roasting pan. Combine salt, brown sugar, and nutmeg. Sprinkle over top of lamb. Roast in a 325° F. oven about 2 hours or to a temperature of 175° to 180° F. on a meat thermometer. Cut lamb in slices and serve with Jelly Sauce.

JELLY SAUCE

about 2 cups

½ cup Currant Jelly
¾ cup water
¼ cup firmly packed brown sugar
6 tablespoons lemon juice

½ teaspoon salt
¼ teaspoon ground nutmeg
⅛ teaspoon ground allspice
⅛ teaspoon pepper

In a saucepan, combine all ingredients. Heat over low heat, stirring constantly, until jelly melts and sauce is hot. Serve with slices of roast lamb.

GRAPE LAMB CHOPS

6 servings

2 tablespoons cooking oil
6 small shoulder lamb chops (1¾ to 2 pounds)
1 medium onion, minced
½ cup ketchup
½ cup Grape Jam

1 tablespoon worcestershire sauce
1 teaspoon salt
1 tablespoon prepared mustard
Hot cooked rice

Heat oil in a large skillet. Add lamb chops; brown on both sides. Remove chops and set aside. Add onion to drippings in skillet;

cook just until soft but not browned. Add ketchup, jam, worcestershire, salt, and mustard. Blend well. Return chops to skillet. Cover tightly and simmer about 1 hour, turning chops occasionally, or until chops are tender. Remove cover during last 15 minutes of cooking time to evaporate part of the liquid. Serve with hot cooked rice.

SWEET-SOUR FISH STICKS *3 to 4 servings*

¼ cup cooking oil
¼ cup lemon juice
½ teaspoon salt
½ teaspoon pepper

2 tablespoons grated onion
1 teaspoon dry mustard
½ cup Currant Jelly
1 pound frozen fish sticks

In a small saucepan, combine oil, juice, salt, pepper, onion, dry mustard, and jelly. Heat gently, stirring occasionally, until jelly melts and mixture is blended. Place fish sticks on a heatproof broiling platter. Brush fish sticks heavily with sauce. Broil about 4 inches from source of heat for 3 minutes. Turn, brush heavily with sauce. Broil 3 to 5 minutes, or until tops are lightly browned and bubbly. Baste once again during cooking time, if desired. Serve with remaining sauce, reheated.

49

SWEET-AND-PUNGENT SHRIMP *3 to 4 servings*

3 tablespoons brown sugar
2 tablespoons cornstarch
½ teaspoon salt
1 tablespoon soy sauce
¼ cup vinegar
¼ teaspoon ground ginger
¾ cup Pineapple Preserves
¾ cup water

1 green pepper, cut into thin strips
1 onion, thinly cut and separated into rings
1 pound fresh or frozen shrimp, cleaned and cooked
Hot cooked rice

In a saucepan, combine sugar, cornstarch, and salt. Add soy sauce, vinegar, ginger, preserves, and water. Cook mixture over medium heat until thickened, stirring constantly. Add green pepper and onion; simmer 2 minutes. Add shrimp, bring to a boil, stirring constantly, and cook until shrimp are hot. Serve immediately with hot cooked rice.

BATTER-FRIED SHRIMP

6 servings

2 eggs
½ cup milk
1 cup all-purpose flour,
  stirred before measuring
1 teaspoon baking powder
1 teaspoon salt
2 teaspoons cooking oil

2 pounds fresh or frozen
  whole shrimp
Oil or shortening for deep-
  fat frying
Orange Sauce (follows)
Grape-Horseradish Sauce
  (follows)
Plum Hot (follows)

Beat together eggs and milk until frothy. Sift together flour, baking powder, and salt. Add to egg mixture; add oil and beat until mixture is smooth and well blended. Set aside. Remove shells from shrimp, leaving tails on. If shrimp are frozen, remove shells under running cold water. Cut partway through lengthwise along outside curve. Lift out vein; wash shrimp and flatten so they stay open. Drain well on paper towels. Place enough oil or shortening to more than cover shrimp in a deep-fat fryer or kettle and heat to 375° F. Dip shrimp into batter, one at a time, and fry, a few at a time, about 4 minutes, or until golden brown and puffy. Drain on paper towels. Serve immediately with Orange Sauce, Grape-Horseradish Sauce, or Plum Hot.

51

ORANGE SAUCE

about 1 cup

1 cup Sweet Orange
  Marmalade
1 clove garlic

1 piece whole ginger root
  or ½ teaspoon ground
  ginger

In a saucepan, combine all ingredients and cook over low heat, stirring constantly, until mixture bubbles. Remove garlic and ginger root. Serve with Batter-Fried Shrimp.

GRAPE-HORSERADISH SAUCE

about 1 cup

1 cup Grape Jelly
1 tablespoon prepared
  horseradish

¼ cup ketchup

Combine all ingredients. Serve with Batter-Fried Shrimp.

Opposite: Batter-Fried Shrimp, Dipping Sauces

PLUM HOT

about 1 cup

1 cup **Plum Preserves**
1 to 2 cloves **garlic, as
desired, very finely
minced**

2 teaspoons **soy sauce**
¼ teaspoon **pepper**

In a saucepan, combine all ingredients and cook over low heat, stirring occasionally, at least 5 minutes, or until garlic is cooked. Remove from heat and cool slightly. Serve with Batter-Fried Shrimp.

Good Idea: With these shrimp and their delicious sauces, try serving brown rice cooked with onion, green pepper, and chopped mushrooms. For dessert, lemon or lime sherbet seems just right—offer some crisp cookies, too.

ORANGE FISH FILLETS

3 to 4 servings

1 pound **frozen fish fillets,
thawed**
½ teaspoon **salt**
⅛ teaspoon **pepper**
3 tablespoons **butter or
margarine**
1 tablespoon **minced onion**
¼ cup **Sweet Orange
Marmalade**

1 tablespoon **lemon juice**
¼ cup **water**
1 tablespoon **butter or
margarine, softened**
1 tablespoon **all-purpose
flour**

Sprinkle fillets with salt and pepper. Melt 3 tablespoons butter in a skillet. Add onion and cook gently until tender. Add marmalade, lemon juice, and water. Bring to a boil. Place fillets in marmalade mixture. Cover tightly and simmer about 7 minutes, or until fish flakes easily when tested with a fork. Remove fish to a heated platter and keep warm. Mix 1 tablespoon softened butter with flour to make a smooth paste. Add to liquid in skillet and cook, stirring constantly, until mixture thickens. Season to taste with additional salt and pepper, if desired, and pour over fish.

HOT PINEAPPLE SAUCE

about 1¼ cups

1 cup Pineapple Preserves
1 tablespoon lemon juice
⅛ teaspoon ground cloves

2 tablespoons seedless
raisins

In a saucepan, combine all ingredients and heat gently, stirring constantly, until well blended. Serve hot with hot or cold baked ham.

ALL-PURPOSE SWEET/SOUR SAUCE

about 1¼ cups

½ cup Apple, Crabapple, or
Grape Jelly
2 tablespoons soy sauce

1 tablespoon worcestershire
sauce
½ cup wine vinegar

In a saucepan, combine all ingredients and simmer 5 minutes, stirring constantly. Serve hot with roast beef, lamb, or pork chops.

Good Idea: Another time, use this sauce hot to dress hot cooked cauliflower, beets, or carrots.

TANGY JAM SAUCE

about 1⅓ cups

½ cup Grape Jam
½ cup Peach Preserves

⅓ cup chutney, chopped
1 tablespoon wine vinegar

Combine all ingredients and blend well. Refrigerate until serving time. Serve with spareribs, shrimp, or egg rolls as a dipping sauce.

APPLE-RAISIN SAUCE

about 1½ cups

1 cup Apple Jelly
2 tablespoons lemon juice
¼ cup seedless raisins
1 tablespoon butter or
margarine

⅛ teaspoon ground
cinnamon
⅛ teaspoon ground allspice

In a saucepan, combine all ingredients and heat gently, stirring constantly, until jelly is melted. Serve hot with hot or cold tongue, ham, or pork.

SPICED APRICOT SAUCE

about 2 cups

1½ cups Apricot Preserves
½ cup water
2 teaspoons lemon juice

¼ teaspoon ground nutmeg
¼ teaspoon ground cinnamon

In heavy saucepan, combine preserves and water. Bring to a boil and simmer 5 minutes, stirring constantly. Remove from heat and add lemon juice, nutmeg, and cinnamon. Serve either hot or cold, or use as a glaze and sauce for ham or roast pork.

HOT MINT SAUCE

about ¾ cup

½ cup Mint Flavored Apple Jelly
2 tablespoons lemon juice

2 tablespoons grated lemon peel

In a saucepan, combine all ingredients and heat gently, stirring constantly, until jelly is melted. Serve hot with any lamb dish.

54 PINEAPPLE TOPPER

about 1½ cups

1 cup Pineapple Topping
⅓ cup chili sauce
1 tablespoon lemon juice

2 tablespoons worcester-shire sauce

In a saucepan, combine all ingredients. Bring to a boil over medium heat, stirring constantly. Use as a glaze and sauce for baked ham, ham slices, or cooked bologna.

SWEET/SPICY SAUCE

about 1½ cups

⅔ cup Grape Jelly
½ cup chili sauce

½ cup sweet pickle relish

In a saucepan, combine grape jelly and chili sauce. Cook over low heat, stirring occasionally, until jelly is melted. Remove from heat and stir in relish. Serve warm or cold with frankfurters.

STAFF OF LIFE

A home heady with the delicious aroma of baking bread offers the warmest of welcomes. Here are fruited loaves, sally lunns, scones and coffeecakes and babas, griddle cakes and muffins, old-time jelly doughnuts—a kitchenful of America's traditional breads. Make them with Smucker's and serve them with Smucker's.

RASPBERRY JAM SCONES

Our British cousins relish hot scones for tea—we enjoy them at breakfast, brunch, or almost any time

2 cups all-purpose flour,
  stirred before measuring
3 teaspoons baking powder
1 tablespoon sugar
¾ teaspoon salt
½ cup butter or margarine
2 eggs

¼ cup milk
¼ cup butter or margarine,
  melted
½ cup Seedless Red
  Raspberry Jam
2 tablespoons sugar

Preheat oven to 425° F. Into a mixing bowl, sift together flour, baking powder, 1 tablespoon sugar, and salt. With a pastry blender or two knives, cut ½ cup butter into mixture to the consistency of cornmeal. Beat together eggs and milk; add to dry ingredients, and toss to mix and form a soft dough. Divide dough in half. On a lightly floured board, roll each half into a 10-inch circle. Place one circle in a 10-inch round cake pan. Spread with half the melted butter, then with the jam. Top with second circle. Spread with remaining melted butter and sprinkle lightly with 2 tablespoons sugar. Bake 20 minutes. Cut into 8 wedges and serve warm.

PINEAPPLE SCONES

2 cups all-purpose flour,
  stirred before measuring
¼ cup sugar
2½ teaspoons baking
  powder
½ teaspoon baking soda

½ teaspoon salt
½ teaspoon ground nutmeg
½ cup shortening
1 egg
¾ cup buttermilk
1 cup Pineapple Preserves

Preheat oven to 425° F. Combine flour, sugar, baking powder, baking soda, salt, and nutmeg. With a pastry blender or two knives, cut shortening into mixture to the consistency of cornmeal. Add egg and buttermilk. Stir until a ball of dough is formed. Turn out onto a lightly floured board and knead until smooth. Cut dough into 8 pieces. Pat each of 4 of the pieces into a circle ¼ inch thick. Spread circles with preserves to within ½ inch of edge. Brush edges with water. Pat out remaining 4 pieces into circles and cover first rounds, pressing edges together. Place on greased baking sheets. Bake 12 to 14 minutes, or until lightly browned. Cut each circle into quarters and serve hot.

Good Idea: Break the scones with your fingers, and butter them liberally. Even though this version is made with preserves, you'll probably want to add more—either the same flavor, or a complementary one, such as strawberry or raspberry. Scones come to us from Scotland, where they are sometimes still baked as they originally were, on a griddle.

CHEESE BLINTZES

10 to 12 blintzes

3 eggs
1 cup milk
½ teaspoon salt
2 tablespoons cooking oil
¾ cup all-purpose flour,
   stirred before measuring
1 pound pot cheese or
   2 cups dry cottage cheese

2 eggs
¼ cup sugar
2 tablespoons lemon juice
Butter or margarine
1 cup dairy sour cream
1 cup Strawberry or
   Raspberry Preserves

In a medium bowl, combine the 3 eggs, milk, salt, and oil. Beat until smooth. Add flour; stir until well blended. Let stand about 30 minutes. To make filling, stir pot cheese with a spoon until smooth. Add the 2 eggs, sugar, and lemon juice; blend well. Set mixture aside. Heat a scant teaspoon butter in a 10-inch skillet. Pour ¼ cup batter into the pan, tilting the pan to spread the batter thinly and evenly. Cook over medium-high heat until batter congeals and sets. Bottom should not brown. Shake skillet to loosen pancake; slide out onto a platter. Repeat with remaining batter, stacking cakes bottom side up as you make them. When all pancakes are cooked, divide cheese filling among them, spreading along one edge of cooked side of each. Turn sides in and roll up tightly, starting with edge that is spread with filling. Repeat, using all of pancakes and filling. Refrigerate about 1 hour. When ready to serve, melt about 2 tablespoons butter in a skillet over medium heat. Brown blintzes carefully on both sides, adding more butter as necessary to brown all blintzes. Serve hot with sour cream and preserves.

SAUCER PANCAKES

6 servings

Some people call these "Dutch Babies"—whatever you call them, they're very good and very pretty

6 eggs
1 cup milk
1 cup all-purpose flour,
   stirred before measuring
½ teaspoon salt

¼ cup butter or margarine,
   melted
1 cup Red Raspberry,
   Boysenberry, or Plum Jelly
Confectioners sugar
1 lemon, cut into 6 wedges

Butter 6 individual shallow casseroles or skillets that are 6 to 7 inches in diameter. Preheat oven to 400° F. In a medium bowl, beat together eggs and milk. Add flour and salt; beat until smooth. Stir in butter. Fill each prepared casserole with about ½ cup batter. Bake 20 minutes. Reduce heat to 350° F. and bake another 5 to 10 minutes, or just until dough is firm. Serve immediately, topped with jelly and a sprinkling of sugar; a lemon wedge should accompany each, to be squeezed over just before the pancake is eaten.

59

SWEDISH PANCAKES

6 servings

A swedish pancake pan can be purchased at a good specialty shop—be sure to follow manufacturer's directions for seasoning the pan

2 eggs
3 cups milk
1⅓ cups all-purpose flour,
   stirred before measuring
1 tablespoon sugar

1 teaspoon salt
Melted butter or margarine
1 cup Blueberry Preserves or
   Blackberry Jam

Beat together eggs and milk. Add flour, sugar, and salt; beat until smooth. Heat swedish pancake pan slowly. Brush with melted butter. Stir batter, pour into depressions in pan, and bake until browned on one side. With small spatula, turn cakes to brown other side. Cakes should be thin with crisp edges and delicately browned all over. Arrange 6 hot pancakes in a circle on a warmed plate and serve hot with preserves or jam.

Good Idea: If you do not have a swedish pancake pan, drop batter by tablespoonfuls onto a heated griddle. Cook quickly. Serve with preserves or jam—for breakfast or lunch, or as dessert after a light dinner. This will make about 6 dozen thin pancakes.

Opposite: Saucer Pancakes, Swedish Pancakes, Griddle Cakes (page 60)

GRIDDLE CAKES

2 cups all-purpose flour,
   stirred before measuring
3 teaspoons baking powder
2 tablespoons sugar
1 teaspoon salt
3 tablespoons butter or
   margarine, melted

1 egg
1½ cups milk
Butter or margarine
Strawberry or Blueberry
   Syrup

Into a medium bowl, sift together flour, baking powder, sugar, and salt. Combine melted butter, egg, and milk; blend well. Pour over dry ingredients and blend until smooth. Preheat griddle until hot. Grease lightly. Drop batter by tablespoonfuls onto greased griddle. When a few holes appear around sides of pancake and bottom is browned, turn and brown other side. Serve immediately with butter and fruit syrups.

Good Idea: If batter is allowed to stand about 30 minutes before baking, it will mellow. Then, when pancakes are baked, bubbles will appear on the surface, which is a signal that it is time to turn the cake.

60

OAT 'N' ORANGE MUFFINS

These moist, chewy-textured muffins will cheer up breakfast on a cold winter morning

¾ cup old-fashioned oats
½ cup orange juice
¼ cup butter or margarine,
   melted
1 cup Sweet Orange
   Marmalade

2 eggs
1 cup all-purpose flour,
   stirred before measuring
2 teaspoons baking powder
½ teaspoon salt

Combine oats and orange juice; let stand 10 minutes. Preheat oven to 400° F. Lightly grease 2½- to 3-inch muffin pan cups. Add butter and marmalade to oats mixture. Add eggs and beat well. Sift together flour, baking powder, and salt. Make a well in the center of the dry ingredients. Pour in oats mixture; stir until batter is mixed but still lumpy. Fill muffin cups ⅔ full. Bake 20 to 25 minutes, or until lightly browned.

CORNMEAL GRIDDLE CAKES

1½ dozen

Serve these to the family along with crisp-fried sausage patties for a super breakfast surprise

2 eggs
1¼ cups buttermilk
1 tablespoon cooking oil
1 cup yellow cornmeal
½ teaspoon baking soda

½ teaspoon salt
Melted butter or margarine
Red Raspberry, Apricot, and
  Boysenberry Syrups

Beat eggs until frothy. Add buttermilk, oil, cornmeal, baking soda, and salt; stir only until dry ingredients are moistened. Preheat griddle. Brush lightly with melted butter. Drop batter onto griddle, using 2 tablespoonfuls for each pancake. Cook until tops are covered with broken bubbles and edges are crisp. Turn and cook until undersides are golden brown. Serve hot with a selection of fruit syrups.

DOLLAR PUFFS

6 servings

¼ cup warm water (105–
  115° F.)
1 package active dry yeast
1 cup milk
2 tablespoons sugar
½ teaspoon salt

1 egg, lightly beaten
¼ teaspoon ground nutmeg
1¾ cups all-purpose flour,
  stirred before measuring
¾ cup Strawberry Preserves
¾ cup dairy sour cream

Into a large, warm bowl, measure water (it should feel comfortably warm when tested on inside of wrist). Sprinkle in yeast; stir until dissolved. Heat milk to lukewarm. Stir milk, sugar, salt, egg, and nutmeg into yeast mixture. Add the flour and stir until well blended. Cover bowl and let stand in a warm place about 45 minutes. Heat a griddle over medium heat. Brush lightly with butter. Spoon level tablespoonfuls of batter onto buttered griddle; puffs should not touch each other. Cook about 2 minutes, or until lightly browned on the bottom. Turn and cook until second side is browned, about 1 minute. Serve immediately with preserves and sour cream.

Good Idea: These good little puffs are equally delicious served with butter and any flavor fruit syrup.

QUICK CARAMEL BUNS

10 buns

½ cup Pecans in Syrup
   Topping

1 package refrigerated flaky
   biscuits (10 biscuits)

Preheat oven to 375° F. Butter ten 2½- to 3-inch muffin pan cups. Spoon about 2 teaspoons topping into each cup, dividing topping equally. Place one biscuit in each cup over topping. Bake 12 to 14 minutes, or until tops are golden brown. Remove from oven and immediately invert muffin pan onto a large piece of foil. Let pan remain over biscuits 30 seconds. Gently remove pan.

BAKED GRAPE DOUGHNUTS

1 dozen

Here's a sweet answer for those who say that they love doughnuts, but can't eat them because they're fried

¾ cup warm water (105–
   115° F.)
1 (13¾-ounce) package hot
   roll mix
¼ cup sugar
1 egg
⅓ cup butter or margarine,
   melted

1 teaspoon grated lemon peel
½ teaspoon ground cinnamon
½ teaspoon ground nutmeg
¼ to ½ cup all-purpose flour,
   stirred before measuring
¼ cup Grape Jam
Melted butter or margarine
Confectioners sugar (optional)

Into a large, warm bowl, measure water (it should feel comfortably warm when tested on inside of wrist). Sprinkle yeast from roll mix over water, and stir until dissolved. Add sugar, egg, ⅓ cup melted butter, and grated lemon peel. Beat until bubbly. Add cinnamon and nutmeg to flour mix from package. Stir into yeast mixture; beat well. Beat in ¼ to ½ cup flour, to make a soft dough. Cover and let stand 10 minutes. Turn dough out onto a lightly floured board; knead until smooth. Place in a greased bowl, turn over to grease top. Cover dough and let rise in a warm place free from draft until doubled in bulk, about 1 hour. Grease baking sheets. Roll dough out to a ½-inch thickness. Cut into 2½-inch rounds. On half of rounds place a heaping teaspoonful of jam. Top with remaining rounds and press edges firmly to seal. Place 2 inches apart on prepared baking sheets. Brush tops liberally with melted butter. Let rise in warm place until doubled in bulk, about 30 minutes. Preheat oven to 375° F. Bake about 12 to

14 minutes, or until lightly browned. Cool. If desired, dust with confectioners sugar.

OLD-FASHIONED JELLY DOUGHNUTS   *2 dozen*

½ cup milk
½ cup butter or margarine
⅓ cup sugar
1 teaspoon salt
½ cup warm water (105–115° F.)
2 packages active dry yeast
2 eggs, lightly beaten
1 tablespoon grated lemon peel

4½ to 5 cups all-purpose flour, stirred before measuring
Oil or shortening for deep-fat frying
1 cup Red Raspberry Jelly
Confectioners sugar

In a small saucepan, heat milk until small bubbles appear at edge; stir in butter, sugar, and salt. Cool to lukewarm. Into a large, warm bowl, measure water (it should feel comfortably warm when tested on inside of wrist). Sprinkle in yeast; stir until dissolved. Add milk mixture, eggs, lemon peel, and 2½ cups flour; mix well, then beat until well blended. Stir in enough additional flour (2 to 2½ cups) to make a stiff dough. Turn out onto a lightly floured board and knead until smooth and elastic, about 8 to 10 minutes. Place in a greased bowl; turn over to grease top. Cover with waxed paper and towel; let rise in a warm place, free from draft, until doubled in bulk, about 1 hour. Punch dough down and knead again on floured board 2 to 3 minutes. Divide dough in half. With lightly floured rolling pin, roll out half the dough at a time to a ½-inch thickness; cut into rounds with a 3-inch cutter. Place doughnuts on ungreased baking sheets. Knead trimmings, then roll and cut as before. Cover and let rise in warm place, free from draft, until doubled in bulk, about 30 minutes. Pour oil 3 to 4 inches deep into a deep-fat fryer or kettle. Heat to 375° F. Drop doughnuts, 3 or 4 at a time, into hot oil; fry 2 to 3 minutes or until golden brown, turning once. Drain on paper towels. Before serving, cut a slit in side of each doughnut. Using a small spoon or pastry tube, fill center of each doughnut with about 2 teaspoons jelly. Sprinkle with confectioners sugar.

CINNAMON-JAM COFFEECAKE

1 cake

3 cups all-purpose flour,
   stirred before measuring
1 cup sugar
1 teaspoon baking powder
1 teaspoon baking soda
½ teaspoon salt
1 cup butter or margarine
2 eggs

1 cup buttermilk
1 teaspoon vanilla extract
½ cup Seedless Red
   Raspberry Jam
½ cup chopped walnuts
2 teaspoons ground
   cinnamon
1 tablespoon sugar

Preheat oven to 350° F. Generously grease and lightly flour a
9-inch tube pan. Into a large mixing bowl, sift together flour,
1 cup sugar, baking powder, baking soda, and salt. With a
pastry blender or two knives, cut butter into mixture to the consistency of coarse crumbs. Remove ½ cup of the mixture and set
aside. Combine eggs, buttermilk, and vanilla; beat together
lightly. Add to flour mixture; stir until well blended. Spread ⅓ of
the batter in prepared pan. Spread half of jam over batter. Combine reserved flour mixture, walnuts, cinnamon, and 1 tablespoon sugar. Sprinkle ⅓ of this mixture over jam. Repeat batter,
jam, and crumb layers. Top with remaining batter, sprinkle with
remaining crumbs. Bake 45 to 50 minutes, or until a cake tester
inserted in center of cake comes out clean. Cool on a wire rack
10 to 15 minutes before removing from pan.

FRUITED PEANUT BUTTER TWISTS

40 rolls

½ cup milk
½ cup sugar
1½ teaspoons salt
¼ cup butter or margarine
½ cup warm water (105–
   115° F.)
2 packages active dry yeast
2 eggs

4½ to 5 cups all-purpose
   flour, stirred before
   measuring
¾ cup creamy peanut butter
¾ cup Peach Preserves
6 tablespoons butter or
   margarine, softened

In a saucepan, heat milk until small bubbles appear around the
edges. Stir in sugar, salt, and ¼ cup butter. Cool to lukewarm.
Into a large, warm bowl, measure water (it should feel comfortably warm when tested on inside of wrist). Sprinkle in yeast;
stir until dissolved. Add milk mixture, eggs, and 3 cups flour.

Beat until smooth. Add enough additional flour to make a stiff dough. Turn out onto a lightly floured board and knead until smooth and elastic, 8 to 10 minutes. Place in a greased bowl, turn over to grease top. Cover and let rise in a warm place, free from draft, until doubled in bulk, about 1 hour. Combine peanut butter, preserves, and 6 tablespoons butter; beat until smooth and set aside. Grease baking sheets. Punch dough down. Divide in half. Roll each half into a 12- × 15-inch rectangle. Cut each rectangle into twenty 3-inch squares. Place about 2 teaspoons of filling in the center of each square. Overlap two opposite corners; seal tightly. Place on prepared baking sheets. Let rise, uncovered, in a warm place free from draft, until doubled in bulk, about 1 hour. Preheat oven to 375° F. Bake about 15 minutes, or until done. Remove from baking sheets and cool on wire racks.

PICTURE-PRETTY BREAD

1 loaf

1 cup warm water (105–115° F.)

1 package active dry yeast

¼ cup Sweet Orange Marmalade or Apricot or Peach Preserves

2½ cups all-purpose flour, stirred before measuring

¼ cup nonfat dry milk solids

2 tablespoons wheat germ

2 tablespoons whole bran

1 teaspoon salt

1 tablespoon cooking oil

Into a large, warm bowl, measure water (it should feel comfortably warm when tested on inside of wrist). Sprinkle in yeast; stir to dissolve. Stir in marmalade or preserves; let stand 5 minutes. Combine 1 cup flour with dry milk, wheat germ, bran, and salt. Add to yeast mixture; stir until well mixed. Stir in oil and remaining flour to make a soft dough. Turn out onto a floured board and knead until smooth and elastic. Place in a greased bowl, turn dough over to grease top. Cover and let rise in a warm place, free from draft, until doubled in bulk, about 1 hour. Turn out of bowl onto a board, knead slightly, and shape into a ball. Let stand 20 minutes. Grease a 9- × 5- × 3-inch loaf pan. Shape dough into a loaf and place in prepared pan. Cover and let rise in a warm place, free from draft, until doubled in bulk, about 45 minutes. Preheat oven to 350° F. Bake 50 to 60 minutes, or until bread sounds hollow when tapped. Turn out onto a rack and cool thoroughly before slicing.

JELLY-GLAZED SALLY LUNN

1 loaf

½ cup milk
½ cup butter or margarine,
  softened
¼ cup sugar
1 teaspoon salt
½ cup warm water (105–
  115° F.)
1 package active dry yeast

3 eggs
3½ to 4 cups all-purpose
  flour, stirred before
  measuring
¼ cup Grape Jelly
2 tablespoons chopped
  blanched almonds
  (optional)

Heat milk until small bubbles appear at edge; add butter, sugar, and salt. Cool to lukewarm. Into a large, warm bowl, measure water (it should feel comfortably warm when tested on inside of wrist). Sprinkle in yeast; stir until dissolved. Add lukewarm milk mixture, eggs, and 3 cups flour; mix well, then beat until well blended. Add enough additional flour (½ to 1 cup) to make a stiff batter. Cover with waxed paper and a towel; let rise in a warm place until doubled in bulk, about 1 hour. Grease and flour 9- or 10-inch bundt or tube pan. Stir batter down and beat well, about ½ minute. Place batter in prepared pan. Smooth surface by patting with lightly floured fingers. Cover and let rise in warm place until doubled in bulk, about 1 hour. Preheat oven to 350° F. Bake 9-inch loaf 45 minutes, or until loaf sounds hollow when tapped with fingers. For 10-inch loaf, reduce baking time 10 minutes. Remove from pan and place on rack. Melt jelly in a saucepan over low heat. Let cool to thicken slightly, then spoon over top of loaf. Sprinkle chopped almonds on top, if desired. Serve warm, in thick slices, with additional jelly. Use a serrated knife to slice, or pull loaf apart into thick "slices" with two forks.

Opposite: Jelly-Glazed Sally Lunn, Breakfast Blossoms (page 68), Orange Marmalade Bread (page 68)

BREAKFAST BLOSSOMS 9 rolls

1 package refrigerated
  snowflake dinner rolls
  (9 rolls)
¾ cup Sweet Orange
  Marmalade

¼ teaspoon ground
  cinnamon
¼ teaspoon ground nutmeg

Preheat oven to 375° F. Grease nine 2½- or 3-inch muffin pan cups. Separate dough into 9 rolls. Separate each roll into 5 even sections or leaves. Place 1 leaf in the bottom of each muffin cup. Stand 4 leaves around edge of cup, overlapping them slightly. Press dough edges firmly together. Repeat with remaining leaves. Combine marmalade, cinnamon, and nutmeg. Place a rounded tablespoonful of the mixture into the centers of each cup. Bake 10 to 12 minutes, or until lightly browned. Cool slightly before removing from cups. Serve warm.

Good Idea: You can also use refrigerated butterflake dinner rolls. Divide dough into 12 rolls. Separate each roll into 3 even sections or leaves. Place 1 leaf in the bottom of each muffin cup, stand 3 leaves around edge of cup, and proceed as above. Or try placing the dinner rolls upright in muffin cups, as directed on the package. Slightly separate tops of rolls and fill crevices with marmalade before baking. For flavor variation, try Peach Preserves with ¼ teaspoon ground nutmeg and ⅛ teaspoon ground ginger, Cherry Preserves with ⅛ teaspoon almond extract, or Blueberry Preserves with ⅛ teaspoon ground cinnamon.

ORANGE MARMALADE BREAD 1 loaf

3 cups all-purpose flour,
  stirred before measuring
4 teaspoons baking powder
1 teaspoon salt
½ cup chopped walnuts
2 eggs, lightly beaten

2 tablespoons cooking oil
¼ cup honey
¾ cup Sweet or English Style
  Orange Marmalade
¾ cup milk

Preheat oven to 350° F. Grease a 9- × 5- × 3-inch loaf pan. Into a large bowl, sift together flour, baking powder, and salt. Stir in nuts. Combine eggs, oil, honey, marmalade, and milk; blend well. Add to flour mixture; stir only until flour is well moistened (batter will be lumpy). Turn batter into prepared pan. Bake 65 to 70 minutes, or until lightly browned and a tester inserted in center comes out clean.

SUPERB BRAN-PRESERVE BREAD *1 loaf*

½ cup all bran cereal
½ cup whole wheat flake
   cereal
¼ cup wheat germ
½ teaspoon salt
2 tablespoons butter or
   margarine, softened
¼ cup Apricot or Peach
   Preserves

½ cup boiling water
½ cup warm water (105–
   115° F.)
1 package active dry yeast
2 eggs, well beaten
3 cups all-purpose flour,
   stirred before measuring

In a large mixing bowl, combine bran and wheat flake cereals, wheat germ, salt, butter, and preserves. Add boiling water and stir to melt butter. Into a small, warm bowl, measure warm water (it should feel comfortably warm when tested on inside of wrist). Sprinkle in yeast; stir until dissolved. Add dissolved yeast and beaten eggs to cereal mixture; stir well. Add flour; stir to make a soft dough. Cover and let rise in a warm place, free from draft, until doubled in bulk, about 30 to 45 minutes. Grease a 9- × 5- × 3-inch loaf pan thoroughly. Stir dough down and spoon into pan. Cover and let rise in a warm place, free from draft, until doubled in bulk, about 30 to 45 minutes longer. Preheat oven to 375° F. Bake 45 to 50 minutes, or until lightly browned. If crust browns too much for your taste, cover with a piece of aluminum foil during last 5 minutes of baking time. Remove from pan; cool on rack before cutting.

Good Idea: Serve with whichever flavor of preserves you use in making the bread to bring out the flavor of both the bread and the preserves.

BLACKBERRY BABA

6 to 8 servings

¾ cup warm water (105–115° F.)
1 (13¾-ounce) package hot roll mix
⅓ cup sugar

6 tablespoons butter or margarine, softened
2 eggs
½ cup Blackberry Jelly

Grease a 6½-cup baba pan or 9-inch tube pan. Into a large warm bowl, measure water (it should feel comfortably warm when tested on inside of wrist). Sprinkle yeast from roll mix over water; stir until dissolved. Add sugar, butter, and eggs. Mix well. Stir in flour mixture from package. Beat well. Place in baking pan. Cover and let rise in a warm place, free from draft, until almost doubled in bulk, 30 to 45 minutes. Preheat oven to 400° F. Bake 30 minutes. (If top begins to brown too much, lower heat to 350° F. for last 10 minutes of cooking time.) In a small saucepan, heat jelly gently, stirring constantly, until melted. Turn baba out of mold onto a shallow pan. Spoon warm jelly over baba at once. Continue basting with jelly until baba has absorbed all of it. Cool before serving.

ORANGE SNAILS

1 dozen

1 package refrigerated buttermilk biscuits (10 biscuits)

½ cup Sweet Orange Marmalade
⅓ cup chopped pecans

Preheat oven to 375° F. Generously butter a 9-inch round cake pan. On a lightly floured board, arrange biscuits in 2 rows of 5 biscuits each. Roll out to a 12- × 6-inch rectangle. Spread with marmalade and sprinkle with nuts. Roll up, jelly-roll fashion, starting at the 12-inch side. Moisten edge and press gently to seal roll. Cut into twelve 1-inch slices. Place cut side down in prepared pan. Bake 15 minutes, or until golden brown. Serve warm.

SURPRISE MUFFINS

1 dozen

2 cups all-purpose flour,
  stirred before measuring
3 teaspoons baking powder
2 tablespoons sugar
½ teaspoon salt

1 egg
1 cup milk
¼ cup cooking oil
2 tablespoons Cherry Jelly

Preheat oven to 425° F. Grease twelve 2½- to 3-inch muffin pan cups. Sift together flour, baking powder, sugar, and salt. Beat together egg, milk, and oil. Make a well in center of flour mixture. Pour in milk mixture. Stir quickly until batter is mixed but still lumpy. Fill muffin cups ½ full with batter. Drop ½ teaspoon of jelly on center of batter. Add more batter to fill cups ⅔ full. Bake 25 minutes, or until lightly browned. Remove from muffin pans immediately.

PECAN STICKY BUNS

8 buns

½ cup Pecans in Syrup
  Topping
1 package refrigerated
  crescent dinner rolls
  (8 rolls)

2 tablespoons butter or
  margarine, melted
¼ cup firmly packed brown
  sugar
½ teaspoon ground
  cinnamon

Preheat oven to 375°F. Lightly grease eight 2½- to 3-inch muffin pan cups. Place about 1 tablespoon topping in each muffin cup. Unroll dough and lay flat on a lightly floured surface. Pinch perforations together. Roll out lightly to a rectangle about 12 × 8 inches. Brush with 2 tablespoons butter. Combine brown sugar and cinnamon. Sprinkle evenly over dough. Roll, jelly-roll fashion, starting at 8-inch edge. Pinch seam to seal. Cut into eight 1-inch slices. Place cut side down in prepared muffin cups. Bake 20 minutes, or until golden brown. Invert immediately onto wire rack over waxed paper. Serve warm.

STRAWBERRY BISCUITS

1½ dozen

2 cups all-purpose flour,
    stirred before measuring
3 teaspoons baking powder
1 teaspoon salt

¼ cup butter or margarine
½ to ⅔ cup milk
¼ cup Strawberry Preserves

Preheat oven to 450° F. Sift together flour, baking powder, and salt. With a pastry blender or two knives, cut butter into mixture to the consistency of coarse crumbs. Stir in just enough milk to make a soft dough. Turn dough out onto a lightly floured board and knead lightly for a few seconds. Roll dough out to a ½-inch thickness. Cut with a floured 2-inch cutter. Place biscuits on ungreased baking sheet. Make a depression in the center of each biscuit and fill with about ½ teaspoon preserves. Bake 10 to 12 minutes, or until golden brown.

LEMON-PLUM TWISTS

1 dozen

1 package refrigerated
    crescent dinner rolls
    (8 rolls)
¼ cup Plum Preserves

2 tablespoons grated lemon
    peel
Sugar

Preheat oven to 375° F. Grease a baking sheet. Unroll crescent rolls and lay flat on a lightly floured surface. Pinch perforated edges together. Roll out lightly to make a rectangle about 12 × 8 inches. Combine preserves and lemon peel and spread over half of dough. Fold remaining dough over to make a 12- × 4-inch rectangle. Cut crosswise into 1-inch strips. Twist each strip lightly. Place on prepared baking sheet. Bake 10 to 12 minutes, or until lightly browned. Sprinkle with sugar and serve warm.

SOMETHING ON THE SIDE

Something crunchy, something spicy, something smoothly sweet, something just a little bit different—there are all these and more in this cornucopia of vegetables and salads and relishes. Try them to perk up any meal. Their old-fashioned goodness, new-fashioned ease of preparation? Both are thanks to Smucker's.

CORN FRITTERS
WITH ORANGE SAUCE

4 servings

1 (10-ounce) package
frozen whole kernel corn,
thawed
Milk
2 tablespoons butter or
margarine, melted
½ cup all-purpose flour,
stirred before measuring

¾ teaspoon baking powder
1 teaspoon salt
⅛ teaspoon pepper
2 eggs, well beaten
Cooking oil
1 cup Sweet Orange
Marmalade
¼ cup butter or margarine

Drain corn in strainer, pressing corn lightly against sides, and reserving liquid. Add enough milk to corn liquid to make ¼ cup. Combine liquid with corn, melted butter, flour, baking powder, salt, pepper, and eggs. Mix until well blended. Pour oil into skillet to a depth of ½ inch; heat. Drop corn mixture by tablespoonfuls into hot oil; fry until golden brown on both sides. In a saucepan, combine marmalade and ¼ cup butter and heat, stirring constantly. Serve sauce over hot corn fritters.

75

YAMS
BAKED IN MARMALADE SAUCE

6 servings

7 medium yams (2 to 2½
pounds)
½ cup firmly packed brown
sugar

½ cup Sweet Orange
Marmalade
3 tablespoons butter or
margarine, melted

Wash yams. Cover and cook in boiling water 20 to 30 minutes, or until tender. Cool. Peel yams, cut into quarters, and arrange in single layer in shallow baking dish. Combine brown sugar, marmalade, and butter, and pour over yams. Bake, uncovered, in a 400° F. oven 20 to 25 minutes, basting and turning yams frequently so they glaze on all sides.

Good Idea: If you're in a hurry, use drained canned yams in this dish—2 (1-pound 8-ounce) cans will work perfectly in this recipe.

Opposite: Yams Baked in Marmalade Sauce, Spiced Beets (page 76)

SPICED BEETS

2 tablespoons butter or
   margarine
1 small onion, thinly sliced
½ teaspoon salt
⅛ teaspoon pepper
½ teaspoon ground
   cinnamon

¼ teaspoon ground ginger
3 tablespoons lemon juice
¼ cup Sweet Orange
   Marmalade
1 (1-pound) can sliced
   beets, drained

Melt butter in saucepan. Separate onion slices into rings. Reserve a few rings for garnish; place remaining rings in saucepan. Cook over medium heat 2 minutes. Add salt, pepper, cinnamon, ginger, lemon juice, and marmalade. Bring to a boil. Add beets, cover and simmer over low heat about 5 minutes. To serve, garnish beets with reserved onion rings.

SPICED CARROTS

4 servings

1 pound carrots, cut lengthwise into thirds
¼ cup butter or margarine
⅓ cup Sweet Orange
   Marmalade

¼ teaspoon ground ginger
¼ teaspoon ground mace
⅛ teaspoon dry mustard
½ teaspoon salt

Cook carrots, covered, in a small amount of boiling salted water until tender. Drain, reserving carrots and liquid. In a saucepan combine ½ cup carrot liquid, butter, marmalade, ginger, mace, dry mustard, and salt. Bring to a boil. Return carrots to pan and simmer about 5 minutes, or until carrots are hot and glazed.

GRAPE-GLAZED BEETS

6 servings

Beets are a neglected vegetable—but served this way, you'll be sure to hear, "Seconds on beets, please!"

2 (1-pound) cans sliced
   beets
2 tablespoons cornstarch
¼ cup orange juice

½ cup Grape Jelly
2 tablespoons butter or
   margarine

Drain beets, reserving beets and liquid. Into a saucepan, measure ½ cup of the beet liquid. Stir in cornstarch, orange juice, and jelly. Cook over moderate heat, stirring, until mixture comes to a boil and thickens. Add butter and stir until melted. Add beets and cook over very low heat, stirring occasionally, 10 to 15 minutes, or until beets are lightly glazed with sauce and heated through.

GLAZED CARROTS

6 *servings*

1½ pounds carrots, cut into ¼-inch slices
⅓ cup Peach Preserves
3 tablespoons butter or margarine

1 tablespoon lemon juice
1 tablespoon snipped parsley

Cook carrots, covered, in a small amount of boiling salted water about 10 minutes, or until tender. Drain thoroughly. Add preserves, butter, and lemon juice, and cook over low heat, stirring occasionally, until butter is melted and carrots are evenly glazed and heated. Sprinkle with parsley just before serving.

GRANDMA'S BAKED SQUASH

4 *servings*

Try this way with acorn squash as a change from the more usual butter-and-brown-sugar seasoning

2 medium-size acorn squash
2 tart red apples, diced
½ cup chopped nuts

½ cup Apple Jelly
¼ cup butter or margarine, softened

Cut squash in half lengthwise; scoop out centers. Place in baking pan. Combine apples, nuts, jelly, and butter. Fill squash with mixture. Pour a small amount of boiling water in bottom of pan around squash. Cover pan with foil. Bake in a 400° F. oven 45 to 60 minutes, or until fork-tender. Remove foil during last 5 minutes of baking.

AUNT MARIE'S
GLAZED PARSNIPS

Sure to bring parsnips back into favor, here's a new-fashioned way with an old-fashioned vegetable

**4 medium parsnips (about
 1 pound), cut into 2- ×
 ¼-inch strips
3 tablespoons Caramel
 Topping**

**2 tablespoons butter or
 margarine
1 tablespoon lemon juice**

Cook parsnips, covered, in a small amount of boiling water about 8 minutes, or until tender. Drain thoroughly. Add topping, butter, and lemon juice. Heat, stirring gently, until butter is melted and parsnips are glazed.

Good Idea: Use this same good glaze to dress up carrots or small white onions.

GLAZED SWEET POTATOES

6 *servings*

78

**7 medium sweet potatoes
 (2 to 2½ pounds)
¾ cup Currant Jelly**

**2 tablespoons lemon or
 lime juice**

Wash sweet potatoes. Place in a kettle; cover with boiling water. Cover kettle and cook 20 to 30 minutes, or until potatoes are tender. Drain and cool. Peel and cut in halves. Place in a 13- × 9-inch baking dish. Beat jelly with a fork until smooth. Add juice. Pour over sweet potatoes. Bake, uncovered, in a 400° F. oven 20 to 30 minutes, or until hot, spooning sauce over potatoes during baking time.

Good Idea: Canned sweet potatoes turn this into a good, quick dish. Top 2 (1-pound 8-ounce) cans drained potatoes with jelly-juice mixture and bake as above.

GRAPE-GLAZED CABBAGE

3 *to* 4 *servings*

**4 cups shredded cabbage
¼ cup Grape Jelly**

2 tablespoons vinegar

Cook cabbage, covered, in a small amount of boiling salted

water, about 6 minutes, or until crisp tender. Drain thoroughly. Add jelly and vinegar and toss lightly with a fork until jelly is melted and cabbage is well coated.

Good Idea: This flavorful cabbage goes well with roast duck or goose—or try it with sauerbraten or sausages.

PINEAPPLED SWEET POTATOES   4 *servings*

3 medium sweet potatoes
  (about 1 pound)
2 tablespoons orange juice

1½ tablespoons butter or
  margarine
⅓ cup Pineapple Topping
½ teaspoon salt

Wash sweet potatoes. Cover with boiling water and cook, covered, 20 to 30 minutes, or until tender. Peel and mash. Add orange juice, butter, topping, and salt; mix thoroughly. Spoon mixture into a greased 1-quart casserole. Bake, uncovered, in a 350° F. oven 20 to 25 minutes, or until hot.

Good Idea: In a hurry? Use 1 (18-ounce) can sweet potatoes. 79
Mash, add remaining ingredients, and bake as above.

RED CABBAGE   6 *servings*

1 small head red cabbage
  (1½ to 2 pounds)
3 tablespoons butter or
  margarine
1 medium onion, chopped
¼ cup vinegar

½ cup water
½ cup Currant Jelly
1½ teaspoons salt
⅛ teaspoon pepper
½ cup seedless raisins
  (optional)

Remove core and shred cabbage coarsely. In a large saucepan, melt butter; add onion and cook about 3 minutes or just until soft. Add cabbage, vinegar, and water. Cover and simmer about 10 minutes, or just until cabbage is crisp tender. Add jelly, salt, pepper, and raisins, if desired; toss lightly. Cook, uncovered, over low heat until cabbage is well glazed and hot. Serve with sauerbraten, pork, or hamburger patties.

Good Idea: Cherry Preserves in place of Currant Jelly makes a very pleasant flavor change.

KRAUT SALAD

1 pound sauerkraut, well
   drained
½ cup finely chopped onion

½ cup Apple Jelly
¼ cup chopped pimiento

Combine all ingredients and toss. Cover and refrigerate several hours, tossing occasionally, before serving.

Good Idea: This can be served as a salad or as a relish. Either way it is just a little different.

ORANGE-PINEAPPLE COLE SLAW

4 servings

2 medium oranges
½ cup mayonnaise
½ cup Pineapple Topping

¼ teaspoon salt
4 cups finely shredded
   cabbage

Peel oranges. Over medium bowl, with a small sharp knife, cut between orange sections. Reserve sections, discard membrane. Add mayonnaise, topping, and salt to juice in bowl; stir to blend well. Add cabbage and orange sections and toss lightly. Refrigerate at least 1 hour before serving to blend flavors.

DATE-AND-CITRUS SALAD

4 to 6 servings

1 (3-ounce) package cream
   cheese, softened
2 tablespoons Sweet
   Orange Marmalade
2 dozen pitted dates
2 medium oranges, peeled

2 medium grapefruit,
   peeled
Watercress or endive
¼ cup Sweet Orange
   Marmalade
1 tablespoon lemon juice

Blend cream cheese with 2 tablespoons marmalade. Slit dates and fill with cheese mixture. Section oranges and grapefruit over a bowl to collect the juice; reserve juice, discard membrane. Arrange dates and orange and grapefruit sections on a bed of watercress or endive. Measure ¼ cup of the reserved juice; blend with ¼ cup marmalade and the lemon juice. Spoon over fruit, toss lightly, and serve.

WHIPPED ORANGE DRESSING   *about 1½ cups*

½ cup Sweet Orange
    Marmalade
1 tablespoon lemon juice

½ cup heavy or whipping
    cream, whipped

Fold marmalade and lemon juice into whipped cream. Refrigerate 30 minutes. Serve immediately with fresh fruit or molded fruit salad.

Good Idea: When you need an emergency dessert, make this quick/easy dressing and serve over pound cake or angel food cake.

ORANGE DRESSING   *about ¾ cup*

½ cup mayonnaise
⅓ cup Sweet Orange
    Marmalade

2 tablespoons lemon juice
½ teaspoon dry mustard

Combine all ingredients and blend well. Refrigerate 30 minutes. Serve with fresh fruit salad.

PLUM CHUTNEY   *about 2 cups*

1 cup Plum Preserves
3 tablespoons wine vinegar
1 teaspoon ground ginger

1 teaspoon ground mace
1 cup seedless raisins
1 cup chopped pecans

Combine all ingredients. Let stand several hours to blend flavors. Serve with cold meats or with curry dishes.

APPLE CHUTNEY   *about 1½ cups*

1 cup Apple Jelly
½ cup seedless raisins
½ cup slivered blanched
    almonds

1 small tart apple, peeled
    and chopped
1 teaspoon lemon juice

Combine all ingredients; let stand at least 1 hour to blend flavors. Serve with cold meats or with any curry dish.

JANEY'S BEET SALAD

6 to 8 servings

1 (1-pound) can diced beets
2 (3-ounce) packages
   lemon flavor gelatin
½ cup Sweet Orange
   Marmalade
1 to 3 tablespoons prepared
   horseradish, as desired

2 teaspoons lemon juice
1 teaspoon minced onion
1 teaspoon salt
1 cup finely chopped celery
Lettuce

Drain liquid from beets. Add enough water to beet liquid to make
1½ cups. Bring to a boil. Dissolve gelatin in hot beet liquid. Add
marmalade, horseradish, lemon juice, onion, and salt. Refrigerate until slightly thickened; fold in celery and beets. Turn mixture into a 4-cup mold. Refrigerate until firm. Unmold salad onto
serving plate lined with lettuce leaves.

PAT'S APRICOT MOLD

8 to 10 servings

½ cup Apricot Preserves
½ cup Pineapple Topping
2 tablespoons vinegar
2½ cups water
1 teaspoon whole cloves

4-inch stick cinnamon
2 (3-ounce) packages
   orange flavor gelatin
½ cup dairy sour cream

In a saucepan, combine preserves, topping, vinegar, and water.
Tie cloves and cinnamon in a small square of cheesecloth and
place in saucepan. Simmer mixture over low heat 10 minutes.
Remove spice bag. Dissolve 1 package gelatin in 2 cups of the
liquid. Stir until dissolved. Pour into a 6-cup mold and refrigerate
until almost firm. Meanwhile, dissolve second package of gelatin
in remaining preserve mixture and stir until dissolved. Refrigerate
until partially set. Whip with a rotary beater until fluffy. Fold in
sour cream. Pour mixture over first layer in ring mold. Refrigerate
until firm, about 8 hours or overnight. Unmold to serve.

Good Idea: This is an all-purpose dish. It can be the main
course of a light luncheon. It can come to the dinner table as a
salad to accompany the meat. And in a pinch—perhaps with an
added dollop of sour cream—it could serve as dessert.

PEACHES HAWAIIAN

6 *servings*

1 (30-ounce) can peach
  halves, drained
½ cup Cherry Preserves

½ cup sliced macadamia
  nuts or almonds
¼ teaspoon ground ginger

Place peaches cut side up in a shallow baking dish. Combine preserves, nuts, and ginger. Spoon preserves mixture into centers of peaches. Bake in a 350° F. oven 15 minutes, or until heated through.

Good Idea: Serve this warm as an accompaniment for roast chicken, duck, turkey, pork, or veal.

GREAT-DAY CRANBERRY SAUCE

about 3 cups

4 cups fresh firm cranberries
½ cup water

1½ cups Sweet Orange
  Marmalade

Place cranberries in a saucepan. Add water; cover and cook, stirring occasionally, until berries pop. Add marmalade and cook about 10 minutes over low heat, stirring occasionally. Refrigerate until well chilled before serving.

APRICOT-HORSERADISH RELISH

6 *servings*

1 envelope unflavored
  gelatine
1 cup cold water
½ cup Apricot Preserves

3 tablespoons prepared
  horseradish
1 tablespoon lemon juice
  (optional)

In a small bowl, soften gelatine in cold water. Set bowl in a pan of hot water; stir until gelatine is dissolved. Remove from hot water. Refrigerate until slightly thickened. Add preserves and horseradish; stir to blend. Add lemon juice, if desired. Refrigerate until set.

Good Idea: Serve this from the bowl with cold roast beef or ham. For a flavor change, use 1 cup Grape Jam instead of the preserves, reduce horseradish to 2 tablespoons, and add the lemon juice.

CAPE COD RELISH

2 tart red apples, diced
2 tablespoons lemon juice
½ cup Sweet Orange
    Marmalade

1 (1-pound) can whole
    cranberry sauce

Combine apples, lemon juice, and marmalade. Break up cranberry sauce with a fork and toss with apple mixture. Refrigerate until chilled.

Good Idea: An excellent accompaniment for any cold meat, or for hot chicken or turkey.

APPLE BUTTER RELISH

about 2 cups

1 cup Cider Apple Butter
½ cup seedless raisins
1 apple, peeled and finely
    diced
1 teaspoon instant minced
    onion

½ teaspoon grated lemon
    peel
¼ teaspoon salt
2 tablespoons lemon juice
½ teaspoon ground ginger

In a saucepan, combine all ingredients. Cook over low heat 5 minutes, stirring frequently. Let stand about 1 hour before serving to blend flavors. Can be served hot or cold.

PEAR RELISH

about 1 cup

1 firm ripe pear, peeled,
    cored, and finely diced
⅓ cup Pineapple Preserves
1 tablespoon grated fresh
    or diced candied orange
    peel

2 tablespoons water
¼ teaspoon curry powder
1 tablespoon vinegar
⅛ teaspoon salt

In a saucepan, combine all ingredients. Cook over moderate heat, stirring frequently, about 8 minutes, or just until pear pieces are tender. Do not overcook. Let stand at least 30 minutes before serving to blend flavors.

Good Idea: Serve this at room temperature or chilled. Good with veal, pork, or chicken.

A BEVY OF BEVERAGES

A cool drink for a warm summer afternoon, a hot one for a nippy day in winter, a hearty beverage to please the after-school crowd, a fruity, festive punch to add the just-right touch to a party—here are all these and more, to suit any taste, any occasion. And each one owes its wonderful flavor to Smucker's.

STRAWBERRY PUNCH

18 punch-cup servings

1½ cups cold water
1½ cups Strawberry Syrup
2½ cups unsweetened
    pineapple juice

½ cup lemon juice
1 quart ginger ale, chilled
Red food coloring (optional)
Ice ring or cubes

Pour cold water in punch bowl. Add syrup, pineapple juice, and lemon juice; stir to blend. Just before serving, add ginger ale. Add few drops of red food coloring, if desired. Float ice ring or ice cubes in punch. Serve immediately.

RASPBERRY PUNCH

18 punch-cup servings

1½ cups Red Raspberry
    Syrup
1 quart sour lemon soda,
    chilled

1 quart ginger ale, chilled
Ice ring or cubes

Pour syrup into punch bowl. Slowly add lemon soda and ginger ale and stir to blend. Float ice ring or ice cubes on top. Serve immediately.

MULLED APRICOT PUNCH

6 to 8 servings

3 to 5 whole cloves
1 cinnamon stick
4 cups water

1½ cups Apricot Syrup
¼ cup lemon juice
1 lemon, thinly sliced

In a saucepan, combine cloves, cinnamon, and water. Bring to a boil. Reduce heat; cover and simmer 30 minutes. Remove cloves and cinnamon stick. Just before serving, add syrup and lemon juice. To serve, place a slice of lemon in each cup and pour hot apricot punch over. Serve hot.

RASPBERRY FROST

25 punch-cup servings

2 cups cold water
1 cup Red Raspberry Syrup
2 (6-ounce) cans frozen
    lemonade concentrate,
    thawed

2 quarts raspberry flavor
    carbonated beverage,
    chilled
Ice cubes
Lime slices

Pour water in punch bowl. Add syrup and stir to blend. Add lemonade concentrate and carbonated beverage, mixing gently. Add ice cubes. Top with lime slices. Serve immediately.

OLD-FASHIONED TEA PUNCH   *12 to 14 servings*

3 cups unsweetened
   pineapple juice
1½ cups strong cold tea
½ cup Apricot Syrup
½ cup lime juice

2 cups ginger ale
Ice cubes
Lime slices
Mint sprigs

In a pitcher, combine pineapple juice, tea, syrup, and lime juice. Refrigerate to chill thoroughly. Just before serving, pour into punch bowl. Add ginger ale and ice cubes. Garnish with lime slices and mint sprigs. Serve immediately.

APRICOT-PINEAPPLE PUNCH   *8 servings*

1½ cups Apricot Syrup
2¼ cups unsweetened
   pineapple juice
½ cup lemon juice

1½ cups cold water
1 quart lemon-lime soda,
   chilled
Ice cubes

Combine syrup, pineapple juice, lemon juice, and water; stir to blend well. Just before serving, add lemon-lime soda. Serve over ice cubes in tall glasses. Serve immediately.

MOCHA HOT CHOCOLATE   *4 servings*

3 cups milk
½ cup Chocolate Flavor
   Syrup Topping
2 tablespoons instant coffee
   powder

1 teaspoon vanilla extract
¾ cup water
½ cup heavy or whipping
   cream, whipped
Ground cinnamon

In large saucepan, combine milk, topping, instant coffee, vanilla, and water. Stir until coffee dissolves. Cook over medium heat, stirring frequently, until hot but not boiling. Pour into cups. Top each serving with a spoonful of whipped cream and a sprinkling of cinnamon.

MINT SPARKLE

8 to 10 *servings*

1 cup Mint Flavored Apple
  Jelly
¾ cup water
2¼ cups unsweetened
  pineapple juice

½ cup lime juice
1 quart ginger ale, chilled
Ice cubes

In a saucepan, combine jelly and water. Heat, stirring constantly, until jelly is melted. Cool. Add pineapple juice and lime juice; stir to blend. Refrigerate until serving time. To serve, slowly blend ginger ale into jelly mixture. Pour into glasses over ice cubes. Serve immediately.

TANGY RASPBERRY FIZZ

8 *servings*

1 cup Red Raspberry Syrup
1 cup Apricot Syrup
1 cup unsweetened
  grapefruit juice

1 cup cold water
1 quart ginger ale, chilled
Ice cubes

In a pitcher, combine syrups, juice, and water; blend well. Gradually add ginger ale and mix lightly. Serve immediately over ice.

PINK LEMONADE

4 *servings*

1 (5¾-ounce) can frozen
  lemon juice, thawed
2 cups cold water

½ cup Strawberry Syrup
Ice cubes
Mint sprigs

Combine lemon juice and water. Place 2 tablespoons syrup into bottom of each of 4 tall glasses. Fill glasses partially with lemon juice mixture; stir to blend. Add ice cubes and fill to top with remaining lemon mixture. Add more strawberry syrup, if desired. Garnish with mint sprigs. Serve immediately.

Opposite: Pink Lemonade, Special Chocolate Soda (page 91)

CHOCOLATE MILKSHAKE

1 serving

¼ cup Chocolate Flavor
 Syrup Topping
⅓ cup milk

1 cup (½ pint) vanilla ice
 cream

Combine all ingredients in container of blender. Cover and process at medium speed 1 minute. Or combine ingredients in a bowl and beat well with a rotary beater. Pour into a chilled glass and serve immediately.

MOCHA MILKSHAKE

4 servings

1 tablespoon sugar
2 tablespoons instant coffee
 powder
½ cup Chocolate Flavor
 Syrup Topping

1 cup (½ pint) chocolate ice
 cream
3 cups cold milk

In container of blender, combine sugar, instant coffee, topping, and ice cream. Cover and process at medium speed 1 minute. Add milk; cover and process briefly. Or combine ingredients in a bowl and beat well with a rotary beater. Pour into chilled tall glasses and serve immediately.

BANANA-CHOCOLATE COOLER

3 to 4 servings

1 large, ripe banana,
 mashed
2½ cups cold milk
½ cup Chocolate Flavor
 Syrup Topping

1 cup (½ pint) chocolate ice
 cream
Whipped cream (optional)

In a chilled bowl, combine banana, milk, topping, and ice cream. Beat well with rotary beater. Serve in chilled glasses; top with whipped cream, if desired. Serve immediately.

CRANBERRY-LEMON FROST

8 to 10 servings

1 quart cranberry juice
 cocktail, chilled
3 cups apricot nectar, chilled
¾ cup Apricot Syrup

¼ cup lemon juice
2 cups lemon sherbet
Mint sprigs

In a large pitcher, combine cranberry juice cocktail, nectar, syrup, and lemon juice. Pour mixture into glasses. Scoop or spoon sherbet into small balls and float on top of each serving. Garnish with mint sprigs. Serve immediately.

BLUE-APPLE REFRESHER
4 to 6 servings

1½ cups Blueberry Syrup
1 cup apple juice
¼ cup lemon juice

2 cups (1 pint) club soda, chilled
Ice cubes

In a pitcher, combine syrup and juices. Stir until blended. Add club soda; stir. Serve over ice cubes in tall glasses. Serve immediately.

QUICK/EASY BEVERAGE IDEAS

APRICOT FIZZ
In a tall glass, combine 2 tablespoons Apricot Syrup and 1 scoop vanilla ice cream. Stir to blend well; fill glass with chilled club soda.

FLAVORED MILK
Stir 2 tablespoons of any desired fruit syrup into a large glass of either cold or warm milk. Sprinkle with nutmeg.

ICE CREAM SODA
Place 2 to 3 tablespoons of any desired fruit syrup in a tall glass. Fill glass ⅔ full with chilled club soda. Top with 1 or 2 scoops ice cream and a dollop of whipped cream, if desired.

MILKSHAKE
In container of blender, combine 2 to 3 tablespoons of any desired fruit syrup, ⅓ cup milk, and 2 scoops vanilla ice cream; cover and process at medium speed 1 minute. Serve in chilled glass.

SPECIAL CHOCOLATE SODA
In a tall glass, combine ¼ cup Chocolate Flavor Syrup Topping and 2 tablespoons light cream. Stir to blend well. Fill glass ⅔ full with chilled club soda. Top with small scoop of vanilla ice cream.

CARAMEL SODA
In a tall glass, combine ¼ cup Caramel Topping and 2 table-spoons light cream. Stir to blend well. Fill glass ⅔ full with chilled club soda. Top with small scoop of vanilla ice cream.

DOUBLE RASPBERRY FLOAT
In a tall glass, combine 2 tablespoons Red Raspberry Syrup, 1 scoop raspberry sherbet, and 1 scoop vanilla ice cream. Fill glass with chilled club soda or lemon-lime carbonated beverage.

RASPBERRY LEMONADE
In a tall glass, combine 2 tablespoons Red Raspberry Syrup and 2 tablespoons lemon juice. Add ice cubes; fill glass with cold water. Stir lightly and serve immediately.

RUSSIAN TEA
Sweeten hot or iced tea to taste with any desired flavor of fruit syrup. Serve hot tea with a cinnamon stick, iced tea with fresh mint.

HAPPY ENDINGS

What's your memory of grandma's kitchen? Jelly roll? Homemade ice cream? Delicate trifle? Creamy chocolate icebox cake? Rows of pies cooling on the windowsill? Plump puddings, festive cakes, airy meringues? Whatever, you will be able to recreate your fondest dreams with the help of these recipes—and Smucker's.

DOWNSIDE-UP CHERRY CAKE

8 servings

¼ cup butter or margarine,
  softened
¾ cup Cherry Preserves
1⅓ cups all-purpose flour,
  stirred before measuring
2 teaspoons baking powder
⅔ cup sugar

½ teaspoon salt
2 eggs
½ cup milk
¼ cup butter or margarine,
  melted
1 teaspoon vanilla extract
Cream (optional)

Preheat oven to 350° F. Spread softened butter in a 9-inch round cake pan. Spread preserves over top of butter. Sift together flour, baking powder, sugar, and salt. Beat together eggs, milk, melted butter, and vanilla. Add to dry ingredients and stir just until mixture is smooth. Pour over preserves in cake pan. Bake 20 to 25 minutes, or until lightly browned. Let stand 2 to 3 minutes. Turn upside down on serving dish. Let stand a few minutes so preserves will drain out over top of cake. Remove pan. Serve warm, with whipped cream, if desired.

JELLY ROLL

10 servings

1 cup sifted cake flour
1 teaspoon baking powder
¼ teaspoon salt
3 eggs
1 cup sugar

⅓ cup water
1 teaspoon vanilla extract
Confectioners sugar
1 cup Blackberry or
  Elderberry Jelly

Grease a 15- × 10- × 1-inch jelly roll pan. Line the bottom with waxed paper and grease again. Preheat oven to 375° F. Sift together flour, baking powder, and salt. In a medium bowl, beat eggs until thick and pale in color. Gradually beat in sugar; continue beating until stiff. Beat in water and vanilla. Mix in dry ingredients and beat just until batter is smooth. Pour into prepared pan. Bake 12 to 15 minutes, or until lightly browned. Loosen edges and immediately turn cake upside down on a tea towel that has been sprinkled with confectioners sugar. Carefully peel off paper. Cut away crisp edges of cake. While it is still hot, roll up cake and towel from the narrow end. Cool on cake rack. Unroll cake and remove towel. Spread cake with jelly and roll up again. Sprinkle with additional confectioners sugar before cutting into slices for serving.

Opposite: Jelly Roll, Aunt Dilla's Jelly-Icing Cake (page 96)

AUNT DILLA'S JELLY-ICING CAKE

⅔ cup shortening
1 cup sugar
3 eggs
2 cups sifted cake flour
3 teaspoons baking powder

½ teaspoon salt
½ cup milk
1 teaspoon vanilla extract
Whipped Jelly Icing (follows)

Grease bottoms of two 8-inch round cake pans. Fit circle of waxed paper in bottom of each pan and grease again. Set aside. Preheat oven to 350° F. Cream shortening; add sugar and beat until light and fluffy. Add eggs one at a time, beating well after each addition. Sift together flour, baking powder, and salt. Combine milk and vanilla. Add alternately with flour mixture, starting and ending with flour mixture and beating well after each addition. Divide batter between prepared pans. Bake 25 to 30 minutes, or until cake springs back when touched lightly with fingertips. Let stand in pans about 5 minutes. Turn out of pans onto rack and cool. Put layers together with Whipped Jelly Icing and frost top and sides of cake with remaining icing.

WHIPPED JELLY ICING

1 cup Currant or Black
    Raspberry Jelly

2 egg whites
⅛ teaspoon salt

Combine all ingredients in top part of double boiler. Cook over boiling water, beating constantly with rotary beater or electric hand mixer, until mixture stands in stiff peaks. Makes enough frosting for tops and sides of two 8- or 9-inch layers.

JAM JELLY ROLL

Could grandma's old-fashioned jelly roll be improved upon? Try this up-to-date version and see!

1 cup Seedless Red
    Raspberry or Seedless
    Blackberry Jam
1 tablespoon all-purpose
    flour
4 eggs

¾ cup sugar
¾ cup sifted cake flour
¼ teaspoon salt
½ teaspoon vanilla extract
Confectioners sugar
Whipped cream (optional)

Brush sides and bottom of a 15- × 10- × 1-inch jelly roll pan with melted butter or margarine. Spread jam over bottom of pan. Sprinkle with 1 tablespoon flour. Preheat oven to 350° F. Beat eggs until thick and pale in color. Gradually add sugar and beat until thick and smooth. Sift together flour and salt; fold into egg mixture. Add vanilla. Carefully pour mixture evenly over jam. Bake 20 to 25 minutes, or until a tester inserted in center comes out clean. Let stand in pan about 1 minute. Turn upside down on tea towel dusted with confectioners sugar. Immediately roll up cake from the narrow end. Wrap towel around roll and let stand until cool. Remove towel and cut roll in slices. Serve with additional jam and a dollop of whipped cream, if desired.

SOUTHERN JAM CAKE   *12 servings*

¾ cup butter or margarine,
   softened
1 cup sugar
3 eggs
1 cup Seedless Blackberry
   Jam
2½ cups all-purpose flour,
   stirred before measuring

1 teaspoon ground
   cinnamon
1 teaspoon ground cloves
1 teaspoon ground allspice
1 teaspoon ground nutmeg
1 teaspoon baking soda
¾ cup buttermilk

Grease a 9-inch tube or bundt pan; set aside. Preheat oven to 350° F. Cream butter and sugar together until light and fluffy. Beat in eggs, one at a time, beating well after each addition. Fold in jam. Sift together flour, spices, and baking soda. Add to batter alternately with buttermilk, stirring just enough to blend after each addition. Spoon mixture into prepared pan. Bake 50 minutes, or until a tester inserted into center comes out clean. Let stand in pan about 10 minutes; then remove from pan to finish cooling.

Good Idea: Some people like a combination of ½ cup Seedless Blackberry Jam and ½ cup Strawberry Preserves in this cake. This nice moist cake keeps well—it really needs no frosting, but you can dress it up with a very thin glaze, if you like.

PUMPKIN MARMALADE TARTS AND PIE

12 servings

Here's a new way with an old favorite to try at holiday time—as a bonus, there is extra filling for a pie that can go into the freezer

1 (1-pound) can or 2 cups pumpkin
1 cup Cider Apple Butter
3 eggs
½ cup firmly packed brown sugar
2 tablespoons cornstarch
1 teaspoon ground cinnamon
¼ teaspoon ground nutmeg
¼ teaspoon ground ginger
1⅔ cups evaporated milk
12 unbaked 3-inch pastry shells
1 unbaked 8-inch pastry shell
¼ cup sugar
½ cup Sweet Orange Marmalade

Preheat oven to 425° F. Combine pumpkin and apple butter; blend well. Separate 2 of the eggs and reserve 2 egg whites. Beat together the 2 egg yolks and the whole egg. Add to pumpkin mixture. Blend in brown sugar, cornstarch, and spices. Add milk; blend well. Pour ¼ cup of the pumpkin mixture into each 3-inch pastry shell. Pour remaining mixture into 8-inch pastry shell. Bake 15 minutes. *For pie,* reduce heat to 325° F. and continue to bake about 25 minutes, or just until set. Cool. *For tarts,* reduce heat to 325° F. and continue to bake 10 to 15 minutes, or just until set. Do not overbake. Remove from oven. Beat egg whites until stiff. Gradually beat in sugar until mixture is very stiff. Spoon 2 teaspoons marmalade over top of each tart. Spread tops with meringue, being sure to seal edges. Bake tarts 10 to 15 minutes longer at 325° F., or until meringue is lightly browned. Cool. Serve tarts, or refrigerate until serving time. When pie is cooled, wrap in moisture-vaporproof wrap and freeze.

Good Idea: If the tarts don't appeal to you, use two unbaked 8-inch pastry shells, and divide the filling between them. Bake both pies until custard is set. Spread one pie with ¼ cup marmalade, then with the meringue, and bake until meringue is browned. Freeze the second pie for later use. When used, thaw at room temperature and top with marmalade and meringue as with first pie and bake until meringue is browned. Or, if desired, serve thawed pie topped with whipped cream.

Opposite: **Pumpkin Marmalade Tarts,** Strawberry-Cheese Pie *(page 100),*
Peach Tarts *(page 100)*

STRAWBERRY-CHEESE PIE

2 (3-ounce) packages
  cream cheese, softened
¼ cup light cream
1 baked 9-inch pastry shell,
  cooled

1 quart ripe strawberries,
  washed and hulled
½ cup Strawberry Jelly

Combine cream cheese and cream; beat until light and fluffy. Spread over bottom of pastry shell. Arrange strawberries, points up, over top of cream cheese mixture. Melt jelly over low heat, stirring constantly. Cool slightly, then spoon over top of strawberries. Refrigerate to chill well before serving. Cut with a sharp knife.

PEACH TARTS

12 servings

Here's an easy-do dessert with a subtle "what's that?" flavor that will have everyone guessing

2 eggs, well beaten
2 cups dairy sour cream
½ teaspoon vanilla extract
¼ teaspoon almond extract

1 cup Peach Preserves
12 unbaked 3-inch pastry
  shells
Toasted slivered almonds

Combine eggs, sour cream, and vanilla and almond extracts; blend well. Fold in preserves. Spoon mixture into pastry shells. Sprinkle tops with almonds. Bake in a 350° F. oven 25 to 30 minutes, or until mixture is set. Refrigerate at least 2 hours before serving.

PEACH MELBA PIE

6 to 8 servings

¾ cup corn flake crumbs
½ cup finely chopped
  toasted blanched
  almonds
2 tablespoons light brown
  sugar
¼ cup butter or margarine,
  melted

4 cups (1 quart) vanilla ice
  cream, slightly softened
½ cup Currant Jelly
1 cup Seedless Red
  Raspberry Jam
1 (1-pound) can cling peach
  slices, drained and chilled
Toasted whole blanched
  almonds (optional)

Combine crumbs, almonds, brown sugar, and melted butter. Press mixture onto bottom and sides of a 9-inch pie plate. Bake in a 375° F. oven 8 minutes; cool completely on wire rack. When cool, spoon ice cream into crust, pressing ice cream to form a smooth, even layer. Cover with foil or plastic wrap; freeze several hours, or until very firm. About 30 minutes before serving, transfer pie to refrigerator for easier slicing. Melt jelly over low heat, stirring constantly; add jam and stir to blend. Arrange peach slices on pie; garnish with almonds, if desired. Pour sauce into serving dish and serve with pie.

RHUBARB-ORANGE PIE

6 to 8 servings

3 eggs, separated
¼ cup butter or margarine, melted
½ cup Sweet Orange Marmalade
2 tablespoons all-purpose flour
¼ teaspoon salt
2½ cups fresh rhubarb, cut into ½-inch pieces
¼ cup sugar
1 unbaked 9-inch pastry shell

Preheat oven to 400° F. In a large bowl, beat together egg yolks, butter, marmalade, flour, and salt. Stir in rhubarb. In another bowl, beat egg whites until foamy. Gradually add sugar, beating until mixture is smooth and stiff. Fold egg whites into rhubarb mixture. Pour into pastry shell. Bake 8 minutes. Reduce heat to 350° F. Continue baking 30 to 40 minutes, or until rhubarb is tender and filling is set in the center. Cool thoroughly before serving.

Good Idea: If you would like a sweeter pie, sprinkle about 3 tablespoons sugar over rhubarb before adding to egg mixture. However, to many people the contrast between the tart rhubarb and the moderately sweet egg mixture is very good. You may also use thawed, drained, frozen rhubarb. If sugar was added when it was frozen, the additional 3 tablespoons sugar would not be necessary.

APPLE-ORANGE PIE

1 (10- to 11-ounce)
package pie crust mix
3 tablespoons butter or
margarine
7 cups thinly sliced, peeled
tart apples

¾ teaspoon ground
cinnamon
¾ teaspoon ground ginger
½ teaspoon ground nutmeg
1 tablespoon lemon juice
¾ cup Sweet Orange
Marmalade

Prepare pie crust mix according to package directions. Roll out ⅔ of pastry to form a 12-inch circle; use to line a 9-inch pie plate. Cover and refrigerate remaining pastry. Melt butter in a large skillet; add apples, cinnamon, ginger, nutmeg, and lemon juice, and cook until apples are tender, about 5 minutes. Remove from heat; add marmalade and toss. Turn mixture into pastry shell. Roll out remaining pastry to form a 10-inch circle. With knife or pastry wheel, cut 10 strips ½ inch wide. Arrange 5 strips across filling; form lattice by weaving remaining strips in opposite direction. Press ends to rim of pie shell, trimming off ends if necessary. Crimp pastry edge. Bake pie in a 425° F. oven 35 to 40 minutes, or until pastry is golden. Serve slightly warm.

Good Idea: You'll need about 2½ pounds of apples to yield the 7 cups called for in this recipe. Greenings, Rome Beauties, or Granny Smiths are good choices. For a nice golden color, glaze the lattice top of the pie before baking with 1 egg yolk beaten with 1 teaspoon water.

STRAWBERRY CHIFFON PIE

1 envelope unflavored
gelatine
2 tablespoons cold water
1 cup Strawberry Preserves
3 tablespoons lemon juice
⅛ teaspoon salt

2 egg whites, stiffly beaten
¾ cup heavy or whipping
cream, whipped
1 baked 8-inch pastry shell,
cooled

In a small saucepan, soften gelatine in cold water. Dissolve over very low heat, stirring occasionally. Combine preserves, lemon juice, and salt. Stir in dissolved gelatine and refrigerate to chill slightly. Fold in beaten egg whites and whipped cream. Spoon mixture into pastry shell. Refrigerate until filling is very firm.

GLACED STRAWBERRY CUSTARD PIE

8 to 10 servings

1 (3¼-ounce) package vanilla pudding and pie filling mix
1 baked 10-inch pastry shell, cooled
8 ladyfingers, split

1 pint ripe strawberries, washed, hulled, and halved
1 cup Currant Jelly
½ cup heavy or whipping cream, whipped

Prepare filling mix according to package directions for pie filling. Cover surface of filling with waxed paper and cool 5 minutes. Pour filling into pastry shell. Cool to room temperature. Place ladyfinger halves, cut side down, spoke fashion from center, over top of filling. Arrange berry halves, close together, cut side down, in circles over top of ladyfingers. Heat jelly over low heat until melted, stirring constantly. Cool slightly. Spoon over berries. Refrigerate at least 2 hours. Pipe or spoon border of whipped cream around edge of pie before serving.

FROZEN STRAWBERRY PIE

6 to 8 servings

1⅓ cups vanilla wafer crumbs
½ cup finely chopped pecans or walnuts
⅓ cup butter or margarine, softened

½ cup Strawberry Preserves
½ cup Strawberry Jelly
1 egg white
1 cup dairy sour cream
Sliced fresh strawberries (optional)

Combine crumbs, nuts, and butter. Press firmly on bottom and sides of 9-inch pie plate. Bake in a 350° F. oven 8 to 10 minutes. Cool. In small bowl of electric mixer, combine preserves, jelly, and egg white; beat 5 to 10 minutes at high speed, until soft peaks form. Gently fold in sour cream. Spoon mixture into prepared shell. Freeze pie until firm; serve frozen. Garnish pie with a few sliced fresh strawberries before serving, if desired.

CREAM 'N' PEACH APPLE PIE　　6 to 8 servings

5 cups thinly sliced, peeled
　tart apples
½ cup Peach Preserves
Pastry for 9-inch 2-crust pie

2 tablespoons all-purpose
　flour
¼ teaspoon ground nutmeg
1 cup dairy sour cream

Combine apples and preserves and toss lightly. Roll out half the pastry; line a 9-inch pie plate. Arrange apples on pastry. Sprinkle with flour and nutmeg. Spoon sour cream over apples. Roll out remaining pastry; place on pie and crimp edges. Cut slits in top crust. Bake in a 425° F. oven 40 to 45 minutes, or until crust is browned and apples are tender. Cool before serving.

Good Idea: You'll need about 6 apples to make 5 cups. Winesaps or MacIntoshes are best in this pie. For a change in flavor, substitute Apricot Preserves for the peach.

DANISH RASPBERRY CHIFFON PIE　　6 servings

The Danes are very fond of raspberry-flavored desserts—here's an up-to-date version of an old Danish favorite

1 envelope unflavored
　gelatine
3 tablespoons cold water
1 cup Seedless Black
　Raspberry Jam
½ cup water

2 egg whites
⅛ teaspoon salt
1 baked 8-inch pastry shell,
　cooled
½ cup heavy or whipping
　cream, whipped

Soften gelatine in 3 tablespoons cold water. In a saucepan, combine half the jam and the ½ cup water; heat over low heat, stirring constantly, until jam is melted. Add gelatine, stirring until it dissolves. Cool just until mixture begins to thicken, then beat with a rotary beater until light and fluffy. Combine egg whites and salt; beat until stiff but not dry. Fold into jam mixture. Fold in remaining jam. Pour into pastry shell. Refrigerate until firm, at least 2 hours. Garnish with whipped cream just before serving.

PINEAPPLE CHEESE PIE

6 to 8 servings

2 teaspoons cornstarch
2 tablespoons sugar
1 cup small-curd creamed
    cottage cheese
2 eggs, separated
2 tablespoons milk
⅛ teaspoon salt

1 tablespoon grated lemon
    peel
1 tablespoon lemon juice
¾ cup Pineapple Preserves
1 unbaked 9-inch pastry
    shell

Preheat oven to 450° F. Combine cornstarch and sugar. Add cottage cheese and blend well. Stir in egg yolks, milk, salt, lemon peel, and lemon juice. Beat egg whites until stiff but not dry. Fold into cheese mixture. Spread preserves over bottom of pastry shell. Pour cheese mixture over preserves. Bake 10 minutes. Reduce heat to 350° F.; continue baking 25 to 30 minutes, or until filling is set. Refrigerate at least 2 hours before serving.

BROWNIE PIE A LA MODE

8 servings

Chocolate lovers, attention—here's the dessert that you've been waiting for

2 cups (1 pint) vanilla ice
    cream, slightly softened
1 (15½-ounce) package
    brownie mix
½ cup chopped walnuts

½ cup Chocolate Fudge
    Topping
2 tablespoons flaked
    coconut

Spoon ice cream into chilled 2-cup bowl or mold, packing it firmly with back of spoon. Cover with plastic wrap or foil and freeze until very firm. Prepare brownie mix according to package directions, adding walnuts while mixing. Bake in 9-inch pie plate. Cool completely. To serve, remove ice cream from freezer. Dip bowl in lukewarm water for 5 seconds. Cut around edge of ice cream with knife and invert onto center of brownie pie. Pour topping over ice cream; sprinkle with coconut. Let stand 5 to 10 minutes at room temperature for easier slicing. Cut in wedges to serve.

SUNDAE PUFFS

6 servings

¼ cup butter or margarine
½ teaspoon salt
½ cup water
½ cup all-purpose flour,
    stirred before measuring
2 eggs

1 (5-ounce) package
    vanilla pudding and pie
    filling mix
2½ cups milk
¾ cup Chocolate Fudge
    Topping

Preheat oven to 400° F. Grease a baking sheet. In a large sauce-pan, combine butter, salt, and water. Bring to a boil. Add flour all at once and cook over medium heat, stirring constantly, until mixture leaves sides of pan and forms a ball of dough. Remove from heat and add eggs, one at a time, beating well after each addition. Continue beating until mixture is smooth and glossy. On prepared baking sheet, form dough into 6 mounds at least 2 inches apart. Bake 30 to 35 minutes, or until puffs are high and lightly browned. Remove from oven and turn off heat. Make a slit in the side of each puff to allow steam to escape. Return puffs to oven and let stand about 10 minutes with oven door open. While puffs are baking, combine pudding mix and milk in a saucepan. Cook over medium heat, stirring constantly, until mixture thickens and comes to a boil. Pour pudding into a bowl, cover with a piece of waxed paper, and refrigerate until chilled. Just before serving, split puffs and fill bottoms with pudding. Replace tops of puffs and spoon topping over each.

107

Good Idea: On another occasion, fill puffs with a favorite ice cream and top with Chocolate Fudge Topping or Strawberry Preserves. To make eclairs as shown in the photograph, shape dough with a spatula on a greased baking sheet into 6 fingers about 1 × 4 inches. Bake same as puffs.

Opposite: Sundae Puffs

CHOCOLATE FUDGE PUDDING   *4 to 6 servings*

This is a new top-of-stove dessert; only rule for success—don't peek while it cooks

1⅓ cups milk	¼ teaspoon salt
⅓ cup sugar	1 teaspoon vanilla extract
¾ cup Chocolate Fudge Topping	4 eggs

Combine all ingredients in the top of a double boiler. Beat with a rotary beater until mixture is very well blended and frothy. Cover and cook over gently boiling water 1 hour. Cook an additional 15 minutes if using a heat resistant glass double boiler. Do not remove cover during cooking time. Serve hot or cold.

GINGERSNAP RASPBERRY PUDDING   *4 to 5 servings*

1 (3¼-ounce) package vanilla pudding and pie filling mix	1 cup gingersnap crumbs
1 cup milk	1 medium banana, sliced
½ cup Black Raspberry Jelly	½ cup heavy or whipping cream, whipped

Prepare pudding mix according to package directions for pudding, using 1 cup milk. Add jelly and stir until well blended. Cover surface with waxed paper. Refrigerate 1 hour. To assemble pudding, use a 3-cup serving dish. Alternate layers of crumbs, pudding, and banana slices, beginning and ending with crumbs, reserving 2 tablespoons for garnish. Refrigerate at least 2 hours. Just before serving, top with whipped cream and reserved crumbs.

PEANUT BUTTER AND JAM CAKE   *12 to 15 servings*

1 (18½-ounce) package yellow cake mix	2 eggs
1 cup creamy peanut butter	1⅓ cups milk
	1 cup Grape Jam

Preheat oven to 350° F. Grease and flour 13- × 9- × 2-inch baking pan; set aside. Combine cake mix, peanut butter, eggs, and milk. Mix according to package directions. Bake 30 to 35 minutes, or until tester inserted in center comes out clean. Cool in pan. When cake is completely cooled, spread jam evenly over top of cake.

DESSERT OMELET

8 servings

6 eggs, separated
⅓ cup pancake mix
⅓ cup dairy sour cream
½ teaspoon salt

2 tablespoons butter or margarine
½ cup Red Raspberry Preserves

Combine egg yolks, pancake mix, sour cream, and salt. Beat until well blended. Beat egg whites until stiff. Fold egg yolk mixture into egg whites. Preheat oven to 325° F. Melt butter over medium heat in a 10-inch skillet with an ovenproof handle. Pour egg mixture into skillet and spread out evenly to cover bottom of pan. Cook over medium-low heat about 6 to 8 minutes, or until puffy and bottom is lightly browned. Place in oven for 10 to 12 minutes, or until knife inserted in center comes out clean. Loosen edges of omelet; slide onto serving plate. Cut into wedges and top each wedge with 1 tablespoon preserves. Serve immediately.

109

BLUEBERRY DESSERT RING

6 servings

1 envelope unflavored gelatine
3 tablespoons cold water
1 cup boiling water
1 cup Blueberry Preserves

1 tablespoon lemon juice
1 cup heavy or whipping cream, whipped
1 cup sweetened fresh blueberries

In a medium bowl, soften gelatine in cold water. Add boiling water and stir until dissolved. Refrigerate until syrupy. Add preserves and lemon juice. Fold in whipped cream. Pour into an 8-inch ring mold. Refrigerate until firm. To unmold, run knife around inside and outside edges. Set in hot water for a few seconds. Invert onto a plate and fill center with blueberries.

Good Idea: When strawberries are in season, use Strawberry Preserves to make recipe, and fill center of ring with sweetened, fresh strawberries. Or, when fresh fruits are not available, serve with thawed, frozen blueberries or strawberries.

MARMALADE-WALNUT BAKED APPLES

6 medium baking apples
½ cup Sweet Orange Marmalade

¼ cup chopped walnuts
¾ cup Red Raspberry Syrup

Wash and core apples. Starting at stem end, peel apples ⅓ of the way down. Arrange apples in a shallow baking dish, peeled sides up. Combine marmalade and walnuts, and fill centers of apples with mixture. Pour syrup over apples. Bake in a 350° F. oven 50 to 60 minutes, or until apples are easily pierced with a fork. Spoon syrup in dish over tops of apples frequently during baking time. Let apples stand 5 minutes. Spoon sauce in bottom of dish over tops of apples once more for a lovely shiny glaze.

Good Idea: If you prefer to let the good marmalade flavor stand alone, omit raspberry syrup and baste apples during baking with a simple syrup made of ¾ cup sugar and 1 cup water, boiled together 10 minutes before using.

110

BAKED APPLES WITH RASPBERRY FLUFF

6 servings

6 large baking apples
⅔ cup Seedless Black Raspberry Jam

1 cup marshmallow fluff
⅓ cup chopped nuts

Core apples almost through to blossom ends. Peel about ⅓ of the way down from stem ends. Place in baking pan, peeled side up. Add enough boiling water to cover bottom of pan. Cover pan. Bake apples in a 350° F. oven 20 minutes. Remove cover and spread half the jam over peeled portion of the apples. Bake 15 to 30 minutes longer, or until apples are easily pierced with a fork. Remove from pan and cool. Combine remaining jam, marshmallow fluff, and nuts; use to top baked apples just before serving.

Good Idea: For best baked-apple results, choose your apple variety wisely. Rome Beauty, York Imperial, Rhode Island Greening, Baldwin, and Newtown Pippin are some of the kinds that bake well, holding their good, plump shape.

Opposite: Marmalade-Walnut Baked Apples

INSTANT DESSERT

6 servings

1 cup heavy or whipping
  cream
½ cup Black Raspberry Jelly
1 teaspoon lemon juice

12 sugar cookies, crushed,
  or ladyfingers or day-old
  sponge cake, cubed

Beat cream with rotary or electric beater until it holds its shape. Combine jelly and juice in another bowl and beat with same beater until mixture is smooth. Fold jelly mixture into whipped cream. Divide cookies among 6 serving dishes. Spoon cream mixture over top. Refrigerate 15 minutes before serving.

PARTY ICE CREAM CAKE

8 to 10 servings

Like a giant layered sundae, here's a dessert to grace any table, warm the heart of any partygoer

½ cup finely chopped
  peanuts
2 cups (1 pint) chocolate
  ice cream
2 cups (1 pint) strawberry
  ice cream
2 cups (1 pint) pistachio
  ice cream
2 cups (1 pint) vanilla ice
  cream

¼ cup Chocolate Fudge
  Topping
¼ cup Strawberry Topping
¼ cup Butterscotch Flavor
  Topping
¼ cup Pineapple Topping
¼ cup finely chopped
  peanuts

112

Sprinkle ½ cup chopped peanuts on bottom of 8- or 9-inch springform pan. Chill pan in freezer at least 30 minutes. Allow ice cream to stand at room temperature 10 minutes, or until slightly softened. Alternate layers of 1 pint ice cream and ¼ cup topping in prepared pan, smoothing ice cream into even layers and spreading topping to within ½ inch of edge. Sprinkle top with ¼ cup peanuts. Cover with foil and freeze at least 6 hours, or until very firm. To serve: remove from freezer, cut around edge of ice cream with knife; remove sides of pan, and place ice cream cake on serving plate. Let stand 5 to 10 minutes for easier slicing.

Good Idea: You may substitute ice cream flavors in this spectacular dessert as you see fit—if pistachio is not available, for example, use mint, or another layer of vanilla. Peach would be delicious, too. Experiment!

CHOCOLATE ICEBOX CAKE   *8 to 10 servings*

18 ladyfingers, split
1 envelope unflavored
  gelatine
1 tablespoon sugar
¼ teaspoon salt
2 eggs, separated
1 cup milk

1 cup Chocolate Fudge
  Topping
½ teaspoon vanilla extract
1 tablespoon sugar
1 cup heavy or whipping
  cream, whipped

Line a 9- × 5- × 3-inch loaf pan with 2 crossed strips of waxed paper, extending paper beyond rim of pan. Line pan bottom and sides with ladyfinger halves, cut sides up. Set aside. In medium saucepan, mix gelatine, 1 tablespoon sugar, and salt. Beat together egg yolks, milk, and topping; stir into gelatine mixture. Cook over low heat, stirring constantly, about 6 to 8 minutes, or until gelatine dissolves. Remove from heat; stir in vanilla. Refrigerate to chill, stirring occasionally, until mixture mounds slightly when dropped from a spoon. Beat egg whites until stiff but not dry; add 1 tablespoon sugar and beat until very stiff. Fold ¼ of the egg whites into the chocolate mixture. Gently fold in whipped cream and remaining egg whites. Pour half of the chocolate mixture over the ladyfinger halves in the prepared pan; add a layer of ladyfinger halves, then remaining chocolate mixture. Top with remaining ladyfinger halves, cut side down. Refrigerate until firm, at least 4 hours, or overnight. To serve, using waxed paper, lift cake from pan to serving plate; gently remove waxed paper. Garnish top with additional chocolate fudge topping.

Good Idea: Use this delicious chocolate mixture to fill a 9-inch baked pastry shell or crumb crust. Chill until firm. Garnish with additional whipped cream and chocolate fudge topping.

FRESH PEACH TRIFLE

6 to 8 servings

1½ cups milk
3 eggs
5 tablespoons sugar
1 teaspoon vanilla extract
1 8- or 9-inch layer yellow
  cake

¾ cup Peach Preserves
1 cup diced fresh peaches
1 cup heavy or whipping
  cream, whipped
Fresh peach slices

In a medium saucepan, beat together milk and eggs. Stir in sugar.
Cook over medium heat, stirring constantly, until custard is hot
and bubbly. Add vanilla and cool. Split the layer of cake in half
to make 2 thin layers. Spread preserves on cut side of each thin
layer. Cut layers into 1-inch cubes. Put half of the cake cubes in
a 2-quart serving dish. Pour half of the cooled custard over the
cubes. Place diced peaches on top of custard. Repeat with remaining cubes and custard. Cover and refrigerate about 1 hour.
Just before serving, top with whipped cream. Garnish with fresh
peach slices.

Good Idea: This recipe can also be made with canned peaches.
Drain a 16-ounce can of sliced peaches, reserving syrup. Dice
peaches. Proceed as above, but pour half the reserved syrup over
the cake cubes before adding the custard.

FRESH PEARS SALINAS

6 servings

*This new version of a classic dessert is just the right conclusion for a company-
coming dinner*

6 small ripe fresh pears
¾ cup Strawberry Syrup

Vanilla ice cream

Peel pears. Cut in half lengthwise and core. In a large skillet,
bring syrup to a boil. Add pear halves. Cover and simmer gently
about 8 minutes, or just until pears are tender. Turn pears once
during cooking time. Place pears and syrup in bowl; cool 15
minutes at room temperature. Place a serving of ice cream in each
of 6 dessert dishes. Top with 2 pear halves and some of the syrup.

Good Idea: For a quick and easy pear dessert, place a serving of
vanilla ice cream in each of 6 dessert dishes, add 2 canned pear
halves and serve with Chocolate Flavor Syrup Topping.

MARIANNE'S BAKED BANANA BOATS

Here's an easy, dressy dessert that you can prepare and cook in 20 minutes flat!

8 large green-tipped
 bananas
½ cup Peach Preserves
1 teaspoon ground nutmeg

½ cup heavy or whipping
 cream, whipped
¼ cup chopped pecans

Slit unpeeled bananas lengthwise along inside curve to within ½ inch of ends and ¼ inch of bottom. With banana on flat surface, slit side up, press ends gently toward center of banana just enough to spread banana open slightly to form a boat shape. Arrange in large, shallow baking dish. Spoon 1 tablespoon preserves over cut surface of each banana. Sprinkle with nutmeg. Bake in a 350° F. oven 15 minutes, or until hot. (Banana skins will darken during cooking.) Serve bananas hot, topped with whipped cream and chopped pecans.

COTTAGE PUDDING

9 servings

¼ cup butter or margarine,
 softened
½ cup sugar
1 egg
1⅔ cups all-purpose flour,
 stirred before measuring

2 teaspoons baking powder
½ teaspoon salt
½ cup milk
1 cup Butterscotch Flavor or
 Caramel Topping

Preheat oven to 350° F. Grease an 8-inch square baking pan. In a medium bowl, cream together butter and sugar until light and fluffy. Beat in egg. Stir together flour, baking powder, and salt. Add to egg mixture alternately with milk, beating well after each addition. Pour mixture into prepared pan. Bake 20 to 25 minutes, or until tester inserted in center comes out clean. Cut warm pudding into 9 squares. Top individual servings with about 2 tablespoons topping.

Good Idea: On another occasion, use 1 cup Blueberry Preserves as topping for this warm pudding.

CHERRY DUMPLINGS

4 to 6 servings

1 cup Cherry Preserves
½ cup water
1 cup biscuit mix

⅓ cup milk
Heavy cream

Combine preserves and water in a 10-inch skillet. Bring gently to a boil. Combine biscuit mix and milk; stir to make a soft dough. Drop mixture by spoonfuls over top of preserves mixture. Cover tightly and simmer 20 minutes. Serve hot with heavy cream.

COUSIN IDA'S DUMPLINGS

4 servings

1 cup all-purpose flour,
   stirred before measuring
2 teaspoons baking powder
¼ teaspoon salt
2 tablespoons sugar
3 tablespoons butter or
   margarine

6 tablespoons milk
1 cup Seedless Blackberry or
   Seedless Boysenberry Jam
½ cup water
1 cup light cream (optional)

Sift together flour, baking powder, salt, and sugar. With a pastry blender or two knives, cut butter into mixture to consistency of coarse crumbs. Stir in milk. On a lightly floured board, pat out dough to a 4- × 8-inch rectangle. Cut into 2-inch squares. In a heavy kettle, combine jam and water. Heat until boiling. Drop squares of dough into kettle. Reduce heat so that mixture is just bubbling. Cover tightly; cook 15 minutes without removing cover. Serve dumplings hot, topping each with some of the hot jam mixture. Serve with cream, if desired.

MERINGUE CUSTARD

8 to 10 servings

6 eggs
6 tablespoons sugar
⅛ teaspoon salt
1½ teaspoons vanilla
   extract
1 cup milk

1 cup light cream
⅛ teaspoon salt
6 tablespoons sugar
½ cup Seedless Blackberry
   Jam

Separate 3 eggs, reserving whites. Combine the 3 egg yolks, the 3 whole eggs, 6 tablespoons sugar, and ⅛ teaspoon salt. Beat until well blended. Add vanilla. Combine milk and cream and heat until small bubbles appear around the edge. Beat into egg mixture. Pour into an 8- or 9-inch square baking pan. Set in a pan of hot water. Bake in a 350° F. oven 20 to 25 minutes, or just until custard is set. Do not overbake. Remove from oven and lower oven temperature to 325° F. Remove custard from pan of water. Beat reserved egg whites with ⅛ teaspoon salt until foamy. Beat in 6 tablespoons sugar, 1 tablespoon at a time, until stiff and glossy. Dot top of custard with jam. Spread meringue over top of jam and custard, making sure to seal edges at all sides of the pan. Bake 15 to 20 minutes, or until lightly browned. Serve warm or chilled.

CARAMEL FLAN

6 to 8 servings

⅓ cup Caramel or Butter-scotch Flavor Topping
1 (8-ounce) package cream cheese, softened

½ cup sugar
1 teaspoon vanilla extract
6 eggs
2 cups milk

Butter a 9-inch round cake pan that is at least 1½ inches deep. Pour topping into pan. Beat together cream cheese, sugar, and vanilla until smooth. Beat in eggs, one at a time, until light. Blend in milk. Pour mixture carefully into pan. Set pan in a larger baking pan. Pour in boiling water to a depth of ½ inch. Bake in a 350° F. oven 50 minutes, or just until set in the center. Do not overcook. Remove from hot water bath and cool on a rack for 10 minutes. With a sharp knife, loosen edge of custard. Invert cake pan onto a large dinner plate with a rimmed edge or a well in the center. Let stand a few seconds. Remove pan and spoon any remaining topping over custard. Refrigerate 2 to 3 hours before serving.

Good Idea: The topping is so tasty and adds so much to the flavor that serving some extra topping, cold or warmed, with the flan makes this good dessert even better.

CHEESECAKE SENSATION

The combination of flavors is what makes this cheesecake sensational—that, and the sink-all-through goodness of the syrup

¼ cup graham cracker crumbs
4 (8-ounce) packages cream cheese, softened
4 eggs
1¾ cups sugar

2 tablespoons lemon juice
2 tablespoons grated lemon peel
1 teaspoon vanilla extract
½ cup Apricot Syrup
½ cup Strawberry Preserves

Butter inside of straight-side casserole or souffle dish 8 inches wide and 3 inches deep. *Do not use a springform pan.* Sprinkle with graham cracker crumbs and shake around the bottom and sides until coated. Set dish aside. Combine cheese, eggs, sugar, lemon juice, grated lemon peel, and vanilla in bowl of electric mixer. Beat at low speed, and as ingredients blend, increase speed to high, scraping the bowl several times. Continue beating until thoroughly blended and smooth. Pour and scrape batter into prepared dish; shake gently to level mixture. Set dish inside a slightly wider pan; add boiling water to larger pan to a depth of about ½ inch. Do not let edge of cheesecake dish touch rim of larger pan. Bake in a 325° F. oven 1½ to 2 hours, or until set. Turn off oven heat and let cake stand in oven 20 minutes longer. Lift cake dish out of larger pan and place on a rack. Let cake cool about 2 hours, or until it reaches room temperature. Invert plate over the cheesecake and carefully turn upside down so cake comes out crumb side up. Slowly spoon syrup over cake. Just before serving, spoon preserves in a narrow ring around outer rim of cake.

RASPBERRY SWIRL CHEESECAKE

1½ cups sugar cookie crumbs
¼ cup butter or margarine, melted
4 (3-ounce) packages cream cheese, softened
½ cup sugar

1 teaspoon grated lemon peel
2 eggs
1½ cups dairy sour cream
½ cup Red Raspberry Preserves

Combine cookie crumbs and butter. Press mixture in bottom and on sides of a 9-inch round cake pan. Refrigerate. Preheat oven to 350° F. Combine cream cheese, sugar, and lemon peel. Beat until well blended. Beat in eggs and sour cream until smooth, scraping bottom of bowl with a rubber scraper during mixing time. Pour mixture into crumb-lined pan. Stir preserves. Place teaspoonfuls of preserves over cheese mixture. Using spoon, partially mix preserves into mixture, creating a marble effect. Bake 35 to 40 minutes, or until set. Refrigerate at least 2 hours before serving.

JEWEL SHOWCASE   *15 servings*

Here's a very pretty, very unusual dessert, just right to serve invited or drop-in friends with a good cup of hot tea

1 cup butter or margarine, softened	**2 cups all-purpose flour, stirred before measuring**
1½ cups sugar	**1 cup Blueberry, Cherry, or Peach Preserves**
4 eggs	
1 teaspoon vanilla extract	

Liberally grease a 15- × 10- × 1-inch jelly roll pan. Preheat oven to 350° F. Cream butter and sugar together until light and fluffy. Beat in eggs, one at a time, beating well after each addition. Add vanilla. Add flour and stir until well blended. Spread batter in pan. To aid you in placing the preserves, mark off top of batter into 15 squares, using tip of knife. Do not cut through batter. Place about 1 tablespoon of desired preserves in center of each square. Bake 30 to 35 minutes, or until tester inserted in center comes out clean. Cool. Cut into squares and serve with additional preserves, if desired.

Good Idea: Although one flavor of preserves will make a delicious dessert, if you use 2 or 3 different kinds, the top of the cake will look very pretty when it comes out of the oven. If you like, serve with whipped cream or ice cream.

BLUEBERRY CREPES

6 to 8 servings

1⅓ cups milk
2 tablespoons butter or
   margarine, melted
4 eggs, well beaten
1 cup all-purpose flour,
   stirred before measuring

½ teaspoon salt
2 tablespoons sugar
Butter or margarine
½ cup Blueberry Preserves
1 cup Blueberry Syrup

In a medium bowl, with a rotary beater, beat together milk, butter, and eggs. Add flour, salt, and sugar; beat until smooth. Let mixture stand 2 hours before cooking. Over medium heat, heat a small skillet, 5½ to 6 inches in diameter across the bottom. Place ½ teaspoon butter in skillet; swirl around pan to cover sides and bottom. Pour in 2 tablespoons batter. Very quickly rotate and tilt pan to spread batter over bottom of skillet. Cook crepe about 1 minute or until it is set and browned on one side. Loosen edges with spatula and turn crepe over quickly. Lightly brown the second side. Repeat, buttering the pan each time, until all batter has been cooked. Stack crepes with waxed paper between if they are not going to be used immediately. Spread about 1 teaspoon preserves over half of the light sides of each crepe. Roll up, starting with the preserve-covered side. Place crepes close together in a baking dish. When all crepes are in the dish, bake in a 400° F. oven 10 minutes, or just until hot—do not overbake, or crepes will dry out. Warm syrup; serve over crepes. Makes about 18 crepes.

EASY "FRENCH" PASTRIES

20 pastries

Delightful little sweets with quick custard filling, and assorted fruit flavors to top them off

1 package refrigerated
flaky biscuits (10 biscuits)
1 (15-ounce) can
sweetened condensed
milk
⅓ cup lemon juice

½ teaspoon vanilla extract
¼ teaspoon almond extract
¼ to ½ cup Pineapple,
Blueberry, Boysenberry,
or Strawberry Preserves

Preheat oven to 375° F. Carefully cut each unbaked biscuit in half lengthwise to make 20 round biscuits. Place each half on an ungreased cookie sheet about 2 inches apart. Bake 5 minutes. Using the bottom of a glass or jar, approximately 1 to 1½ inches in diameter, press down the centers of the partially baked biscuits, forming a ridge around the outside edge. Return to oven and bake 4 minutes longer, or until biscuits are lightly browned. Remove biscuits from pan and cool thoroughly. In a bowl, combine condensed milk, lemon juice, and vanilla and almond extracts. Stir until well blended and thickened. Spoon mixture into cooled biscuits. Refrigerate at least 30 minutes. Top each biscuit with ½ to 1 teaspoon desired preserves.

CARAMEL CUSTARDS

6 servings

6 tablespoons Caramel
Topping
4 eggs
¼ cup sugar

1 teaspoon vanilla extract
¼ teaspoon salt
2 cups milk

Butter six 6-ounce custard cups. Place 1 tablespoon topping into each cup. Place cups in a 13- × 9- × 2-inch baking pan. Combine eggs, sugar, vanilla, and salt, and beat until well blended. Gradually add milk and blend. Pour mixture into prepared custard cups. Pour hot water into baking pan to a depth of ¾ inch. Bake in a 300° F. oven 1 hour, or until knife inserted in center of custard comes out clean. Remove cups from pan and cool slightly on rack. Refrigerate at least 4 hours, or overnight. To serve, cut around edge of custard with a knife and invert onto a dessert dish.

STRAWBERRY ICE CREAM

about 1½ quarts

1½ cups milk
1 tablespoon cornstarch
⅛ teaspoon salt
2 eggs

1 cup Strawberry Syrup
½ cup Strawberry Preserves
1½ cups heavy or whipping cream

In a saucepan, combine milk and cornstarch. Cook over moderate heat, stirring constantly, until mixture comes to a boil. Simmer 1 minute. Beat salt and eggs together. Stirring constantly, add about half of the hot milk mixture to eggs. Return mixture to saucepan. Cook over low heat, stirring constantly, for 1 minute. Remove from heat and stir in syrup and preserves. Refrigerate about 1 hour, or until chilled. Stir in heavy cream. Process according to directions accompanying your ice cream freezer.

Good Idea: For a change of flavor, omit Strawberry Preserves and Syrup; substitute Seedless Red Raspberry Jam and Red Raspberry Syrup. And, for a quick treat on a day when you're in a hurry, have a sundae party with vanilla ice cream from the store, served with a selection of several syrups and toppings.

NUTTED GRAPE SAUCE

about 1½ cups

½ cup Grape Jam
1 tablespoon lemon juice
½ cup Pineapple Topping

½ cup chopped pecans or peanuts

In a saucepan, combine jam, lemon juice, and topping. Cook over low heat, stirring constantly, until jam melts. Remove from heat and cool. Stir in nuts. Serve over cake squares with ice cream.

GRAPE DESSERT SAUCE

about 3 cups

2 cups Grape Jelly
½ cup Apricot Syrup
½ cup orange juice

2 teaspoons lemon juice
¼ teaspoon ground nutmeg

In a saucepan, combine all ingredients. Cook over low heat, stirring constantly, until jelly is melted. Serve warm over ice cream, cake squares, pancakes, or waffles.

Opposite: Sundae Party—Vanilla Ice Cream with a selection of Smucker's Toppings

RASPBERRY SAUCE

about 1 cup

**1 cup Seedless Red
Raspberry Jam**

**⅛ teaspoon salt
2 teaspoons lemon juice**

Place jam in a saucepan. Cook over low heat, stirring constantly, until melted. Remove from heat and stir in salt and lemon juice. Cool slightly. Serve warm over ice cream.

Good Idea: For a Peach Melba, place a peach half on top of a scoop of vanilla ice cream. Spoon warm Raspberry Sauce over the top. Or serve a slice of sponge cake or pound cake (toasted, if you like) with a scoop of vanilla ice cream topped with Raspberry Sauce.

FRUIT MALLOW SAUCE

about 1 cup

**½ cup Blueberry or
Boysenberry Syrup**
**½ cup miniature
marshmallows**

**¼ teaspoon almond extract
1 egg white**

In a saucepan, combine syrup and marshmallows; cook over low heat, stirring occasionally, until marshmallows are melted. Continue cooking 3 to 4 minutes. Remove from heat and add almond extract. Beat egg white until stiff; gradually add syrup mixture and beat until well blended.

Good Idea: Serve warm over ice cream, angel food cake, or fruit.

TROPICAL SAUCE

about 2 cups

**1 cup Pineapple Topping
1 cup Strawberry Topping**

**1 teaspoon lemon juice
½ cup flaked coconut**

In a bowl, combine all ingredients; stir until well blended.

Good Idea: This is excellent served, at room temperature, over ice cream or sherbet. Or warm the sauce very gently and serve on slices of plain cake, or over split ladyfingers.

USE OF METRIC IN COOKING

COMMON EQUIVALENTS:

Liquid Ingredients
1 teaspoon = 5 milliliters = ⅙ fluid ounce
3 teaspoons = 15 milliliters = 1 tablespoon = ½ fluid ounce
16 tablespoons = 237 milliliters = 1 cup = 8 fluid ounces
2 cups = 473 milliliters = 1 pint = 16 fluid ounces
1 fluid ounce = 30 milliliters
1 quart = .946 liter or approximately 1 liter

Dry or Solid Ingredients
1 ounce by weight = 28 grams
1 pound (16 ounces) = 454 grams

WEIGHTS OF COMMON INGREDIENTS:
Most recipe ingredients vary in specific gravity. Because of this, for example,
1 cup flour does not weigh as much as 1 cup sugar. Below are some of the more
common ingredients used in recipes with an approximate weight for the specified
unit of measure.

Ingredient	Unit of Measure	Approximate Weight in Grams
Butter	1 cup	224 grams
Corn syrup	1 cup	328 grams
Crumbs, bread, soft	1 cup	46 grams
bread, dry	1 cup	113 grams
graham cracker	1 cup	86 grams
Egg	1 medium	41 grams
Eggs	1 cup	248 grams
Flour, all-purpose, sifted	1 cup	115 grams
all-purpose, unsifted	1 cup	125 grams
cake, sifted	1 cup	96 grams
Honey	1 cup	332 grams
Jam	1 cup	340 grams
Jelly	1 cup	283 grams
Ketchup	1 cup	273 grams
Maple syrup	1 cup	312 grams
Milk, whole or skim	1 cup	242 grams
Molasses	1 cup	309 grams
Oats, quick-cooking	1 cup	72 grams

Ingredient	Unit of Measure	Approximate Weight in Grams
Oil, cooking	1 cup	210 grams
Peanut butter	1 cup	251 grams
Pecans or walnuts, chopped	1 cup	118 grams
Preserves	1 cup	340 grams
Shortening, vegetable	1 cup	188 grams
Sugar, granulated	1 cup	200 grams
brown	1 cup	200 grams
confectioners, sifted	1 cup	95 grams
Topping, ice cream	1 cup	340 grams
Water	1 cup	237 grams
Baking powder	1 teaspoon	4.1 grams
Baking soda	1 teaspoon	4.0 grams
Cornstarch	1 teaspoon	3.0 grams
Salt	1 teaspoon	6.0 grams

INDEX

128